ERNEST C. WITHERS
THE MEMPHIS BLUES AGAIN

ERNEST C. WITHERS
THE MEMPHIS BLUES AGAIN

SIX DECADES
OF MEMPHIS MUSIC
PHOTOGRAPHS

SELECTED AND WITH TEXT
BY DANIEL WOLFF

VIKING STUDIO

VIKING STUDIO

Published by the Penguin Group
Penguin Putnam Inc., 375 Hudson Street,
New York, New York 10014, U.S.A.
Penguin Books Ltd, 27 Wrights Lane,
London W8 5TZ, England
Penguin Books Australia Ltd, Ringwood,
Victoria, Australia
Penguin Books Canada Ltd, 10 Alcorn Avenue,
Toronto, Ontario, Canada M4V 3B2
Penguin Books (N.Z.) Ltd, 182-190 Wairau Road,
Auckland 10, New Zealand

Penguin Books Ltd, Registered Offices:
Harmondsworth, Middlesex, England

First published in 2001 by Viking Studio,
a member of Penguin Putnam Inc.

10 9 8 7 6 5 4 3 2 1

Photographs courtesy of Panopticon Gallery, Waltham, Massachusetts

ISBN 0-670-03031-7

Editor: Christopher Sweet
Assistant Editor: Michelle Li
Managing Editor: Tory Klose
Production Manager: Ellen Schiller
Design by: Jaye Zimet

CIP data available

Printed in Japan

Frontis: **Isaac Hayes** in his Stax
office, 1970s.

For my wife, Dorothy
E.C.W.

For Amos and Lorenzo
D. W.

Acknowledgments

I am most grateful for the golden opportunity to serve the legacy of Beale Street as one of the first black policemen, a military-trained photographer, and a historian. I have been given the glorious appointment of husband for sixty years to my wonderful wife, Dorothy, who unselfishly presented me with seven sons and one daughter: Ernest Jr., Perry, Billy, Wendell, Teddy, Daryl, Rome and Rozz. I have been undergirded professionally by my assistant and friend, Richard Jones, for the last thirty-five years.

It would be remiss of me not to mention John Elkington of Performa Entertainment Reality Inc.; executive director of the Beale Street Merchant Association, Rickey Pete; Lieutenant George W. Lee; Sunbeam and Ernestine Mitchell; Walter and Hattie Culpepper; and the legacy of Johnny Mills's barbecue.

The great memory of W. C. Handy, "Memphis Beale Street Blues" and "The St. Louis Blues" will forever be a treasure indelibly etched in my memory. Mr. Robert Henry, Nat D. Williams, Mr. Barasso of The Palace Theater also leave footprints in the sand of Beale Street.

I'll never forget Rob Wright, who suggested the idea of WDIA to Burt Ferguson. Fess Hulbert and Gatemouth Moore bring to the forefront other industries such as the Coca-Cola Club, the Hotel Men's Improvement Club, The Hippodrome, Club Handy, the Mandarin Inn and the Masonic Temple.

What would Beale Street have been without the emergence of B. B. King, Elvis Presley, Bobby Blue Bland, Johnny Ace, Dub Jenkins and Jimmy Lunceford's band.

Memphis, which houses Beale Street, is the birthplace of Aretha Franklin, Booker T. Little, Willie Mitchell, Phineas and Calvin Newborn, the Steinbergs, Frank Strozier and Isaac Hayes, to name a few.

Sometimes in the cool of a progressing Beale Street evening I can still hear Charles Robinson play "Close Your Eyes" at the Barn Night Club and The Silver Moon. Charles and Andrew Perry used to wait around the corner for service to end at the First Baptist Church Beale Street so they could play that music loud.

I also pay musical tribute to trumpet player Mickey Gregory and saxophone player Herman Green. I'll always remember my two personal assistants, Beverly Watkins and Shirley Herron Alexander, who accompany me whenever possible and never forgot my birthday.

And to Tony Decaneas, my agent and dear friend, whose lab and gallery in Massachusetts, Panopticon, handles all of my fine art requests and printing with the help of his friendly staff, Laura Lakeway, Paul Sneyd and Mark Sandrof.   **E.C.W.**

Many thanks to Marta Renzi; to Ernest and Dorothy Withers; to the folks at Panopticon; to our editor at Viking Studio, Christopher Sweet, and his colleagues, particularly Michelle Li; to various experts who have helped with identification (although I, unfortunately, must take full responsibility for all errors), including Rob Bowman, John James Broven, Jim Cole, Charlie Gillett, Robert Gordon, Andrea Lisle, Kip Lornell, Greil Marcus, Dave Marsh, Charles McGovern, Eric Nisenson, Jimmy Ogle and the Rock and Soul Museum, Deannie Parker and the Soulsville Museum, Tony Scherman, John Sinclair, Robert Taplin, and Dick Waterman; and to Cozy Corner for the ribs.   **D.W.**

Lionel Hampton,
The Hippodrome, mid-1950s.

Ask the photographer Ernest Withers
what he listens to when he gets home, and he'll tell you: "I don't deal in relaxation music. I deal in news."

Wait a second. Before us is a collection of Withers's photographs that spans six decades: jug bands to jazz crooners to gospel choirs to funk orchestras. Over here's a picture of what looks like an outdoor burlesque show complete with dancing girls and honking saxophones. And there, from thirty years later, is a close-up of singer Al Green, eyes closed, burrowing for the kind of deep soul that made hit songs like "Let's Stay Together." These pictures—and the gorgeous shots of the young Ike and Tina Turner, Elvis Presley, and Isaac Hayes—are great to see, but they're about entertainment, amusement, relaxation, not news.

Or are they? Ernest Withers has been a commercial photographer on and around Beale Street in Memphis, Tennessee, since the end of World War Two. He's supported himself, his wife Dorothy, and their eight children by covering everything from funerals to civil rights marches to Al Green concerts. In that way, these music photographs are, indeed, news. Withers made them to do a specific job: to tell us, for example, who was playing in which Memphis club when. Ask the photographer what he wanted to accomplish with his work, and Withers's response is: "I'm authentic. My presence will reflect what I saw and what went on." Ask him if he ever aimed to be an historian, and he'll deny it emphatically: "No, no, no, no! It was just a matter of taking pictures." Ask Withers about his skills, and he'll tell you he learned what he calls "finite viewing" from his mother, a seamstress: "She'd send me to the store with ten,

twelve, fifteen pieces of material to buy thread, and I had to match the thread. That gave me the sensitivity for viewing people. In a finite sense."

Okay, then, these are news photographs. And maybe we can attribute their glorious light and the exactitude with which they capture their subjects to the photographer's "finite viewing." But just as we settle into the idea that we're looking at journalism, a strange thing happens. It starts with the smallest details. How the legendary gospel composer, Lucy Campbell, leans a little sideways at the piano. Or the way Aretha Franklin looks into her father's eyes. Soon, these bits of information begin to connect to each other, answer and echo each other, until we have to wonder: What exactly is the news?

At that point, it may help to check out Withers's portrait of R & B star Roy Brown, mugging it up on stage. Or, more accurately, it may help to remember the chorus to his classic song: "Have you heard the news? There's good rockin' tonight." If you've ever listened to Brown, or Wynonie Harris, or Elvis Presley sing those words, you know that the news they announce is more than just who's playing at the Palace Theater. What they're singing about is a kind of wild possibility and hope. *That* is what Withers brings us here: the constantly breaking news of people creating culture, making lasting beauty, and, yes, having fun. The slogan on Withers's business card reads, "Pictures Tell the Story." It's only by absorbing the long, complex, interconnected story his work lays out that we can begin to comprehend just how big the news is.

In 1946, when Ernest Withers was discharged from the army, he joined the ranks of millions of veterans who were returning home eager to work, to make up for lost time, and to reap the benefits of the freedom for which they'd been fighting. Withers came back to his native Memphis to make his living as a photographer, using the skills he'd refined in his three years with the 1319 Engineering Regiment. Age twenty-four, with a wife and family to support, he set up shop in the northern part of the city. As a Negro, Withers had no choice about his clients and subject matter. "This is the black side of life," he says of his work. "I never shot a total of a hundred white people in a whole five years back then. Because I didn't come in white society." Memphis and "Boss" Crump made sure of that.

Edward Hall Crump, a strict segregationist, had been elected mayor of Memphis in 1909, thirteen years before Withers was born. The political machine that Crump put together would maintain control of the city even beyond his death in 1954. His tactic was to isolate the Negro population in a city-within-a-city centered around the famous Beale Street. By the 1920s, Memphis was known as the nation's "murder capital": a wide-open metropolis of 150,000 with 500 saloons. While most of Beale was white-owned, and both the shows and the whorehouses admitted white visitors, Crump was quick to suppress even the suggestion of integration. "You have a bunch of niggers teaching social equality, teaching social hatred," Crump told the editor of the *Memphis World* in 1940. "I am not going to stand for it. I've dealt with niggers all my life, and I know how to treat them."

Withers had learned the rules of Crump's Memphis early on. As a boy, he'd had a paper route that earned him fifteen cents a day. "This woman would see me coming," he recalls, "and stop me on the white side [of the street] to bring her her paper. So she wouldn't have to go on

Reverend C. L. Franklin and his daughter, **Aretha,** SCLC Convention, Club Paradise, July 1968.

the black side. One day, I volunteered and come in the white side before she begged me. And that woman took that paper," he says, chuckling, "and whupped me out!"

If he can laugh about it now, there was a time when Withers considered joining the millions of his fellow Negroes trying to escape this Southern brand of racism. "The avenue for greatness for African Americans," he recalls, "was always from Memphis to Detroit, Memphis to Chicago, Memphis to Cleveland." One friend advised him, "Chicago is as near paradise as a black man gets!" and, as a young man, he hopped freight there in the hope of enrolling in photography school. But his native city drew him back, and, as it turned out, the photographer picked a prime location: in the coming decades, Memphis would emerge as one of the epicenters of black culture in general and popular music in particular.

Withers describes what he did those first years back from the army as: "showing up at public events with a camera." Inevitably, he ran into Nat D. Williams, a teacher at Booker T. Washington High School and one of the leading Negro journalists in Memphis. "Nat Williams," says Withers, "mentored everybody. He trained everybody that he came in contact with, as students and as people." Nat Dee, instantly recognizable by his thick glasses and broad grin, was always promoting one event or another and immediately saw the potential in Withers. "He was just like a farmer with a dairy cow," says the photographer. "He fed you well and milked you well. Put in you what he needed and got out of you what he needed."

At the time, Withers didn't own an automobile, so Nat Dee would pick him up and bring him to public events, such as the amateur night Williams emceed at the Palace Theater. In Withers's words, "He commenced to train me. . . . I guess I was well built in terms of ideology, but I didn't have the maturity he had. He didn't say [what to shoot] image by image, but he went on to teach you excitement, the desires of after-moments, the recording of what went on, the 1-2-3-4 of the importance of any day." At that time, Withers notes, "Being commissioned or hired was kind of a nod. And being paid was kind of a struggle." Still, one of the ironies of the city's segregation was it guaranteed a market for his images. White papers didn't cover Beale Street, which meant that within his community, Withers says, "Anything that you chronicled or recorded was always news. It wasn't going to be seen nowhere else."

Often, that news centered around music. As the cotton capital of the region, Memphis had for nearly a century drawn rural blacks seeking opportunities and possibilities. Along with the people came their music. It ranged from preachers singing on the street corners to string bands with their tipsy off-rhythms to more formal black orchestras. Touring shows like F. S. Walcott's Rabbit Foot Minstrels played Beale in the 1920s and 30s, and their stars—Ma Rainey, Bessie Smith—influenced generations to come. At the same time, Memphis had a tradition of musical education that came to be symbolized by W. C. Handy. Handy earned his title as "Father of the Blues" by transcribing a sharecropper's moan and turning it into a campaign song, "Mister Crump's Blues" (later popular as "The Memphis Blues"). Handy was a strict bandleader whose orchestra followed carefully written arrangements. As Withers proudly puts it: "W. C. Handy wasn't no hang-out floppy-dop. W. C. Handy was a man of true thought. He didn't take no frivolous conversation. W. C. Handy was a trained musician."

The city's musical mix also included a strong church tradition. "Black gospel," says Withers, "was always harmonious and emotional, parallel to blues and rhythm." At the turn of the century, Bishop C. H. Mason established the Church of God in Christ (COGIC) in Memphis. Its sanctified music featured a driving, ecstatic beat that was the Sunday morning equivalent of the Saturday night blues. In 1919, a young high school teacher, Ms. Lucy Campbell, became the first woman of color to publish a religious song of her own composition. She would go on to lead the historical transition from the Negro spiritual to the modern gospel song, writing classics such as "In the Upper Room" and "He Understands; He'll Say 'Well Done.'" By the mid-1920s, another great gospel composer, Reverend W. Herbert Brewster, Sr., would move to Memphis. From his East Trigg Baptist church, he'd stage elaborate gospel pageants and introduce songs that swept through black America. "Reverend Brewster," notes Withers, "had a divine church. You could enjoy the music, but you couldn't get off track by smoking and drinking."

Withers's photography business was hard going, especially in those early years. In 1948, when one of the city's well-paying and prestigious jobs suddenly opened to Negroes, he jumped at it. That year, Crump had refused to allow the Freedom Train to stop in Memphis. The train was touring the country with a display of historical documents, including the original Declaration of Independence and Bill of Rights, but

Crump told the papers he was concerned about: "Whites and colored, men and women and children, surging through at the same time . . . A custom of a hundred and fifty years can't be sidetracked in a day or a year and made workable." The subsequent outrage helped defeat Crump's candidate in the 1948 U.S. Senate primary. During the same period, long-simmering resentment of the all-white Memphis police force boiled over after a policeman shot an unarmed Negro veteran. In the end, all these political pressures forced Crump to allow a small group of young blacks to begin police training, and Withers was one of them.

For a while, photography was his weekend job. "Once you became a policeman and a photographer," Withers soon discovered, "you had a double whammy." He found himself with improved access to the Beale Street clubs (where his white superiors on the force controlled the after-hours bootlegging). Withers would regularly spend Saturday nights at the Hippodrome or the Club Paradise, making the connection between what he calls, "good times and money." For a dollar and a half, he'd take portraits of audience members celebrating their night on the town. "I was there," Withers says with a chuckle, "being seen, making pictures. You're always out to make money. I used to make forty, fifty, sixty dollars a night, maybe a hundred."

He also took portraits of the performers. If Count Basie had a show at the Beale Street Auditorium, the bandleader might then go over to an after-hours jam session at the Hotel Men's Improvement Club. There, Withers would make his picture. "Becoming a new photographer, you didn't get busy worrying about selling," he remembers. "You worried about having." He'd then display the portrait in his shop. "People came in and saw them and decided to [use you] to do promotions later on, decided that they wanted what you had. People always like stars," he adds. "People always care for stars."

Negro police officers weren't the only sign of change in Memphis. The same year Withers joined the force, local radio station WDIA became the nation's first to feature all-black programming. It didn't come about through any sense of injustice, Withers notes: the station's white owners turned to the Negro market in a last ditch effort to avoid bankruptcy. But as a result, in the midst of Boss Crump's segregated city, WDIA began broadcasting the best in black music—gospel and secular—to anyone who cared to listen. The teenage Elvis Presley could tune in from his all-white, low-income housing unit, and, across town, so could Isaac Hayes, who remembers the moment of "Wow! A black man on the radio." The black man in question was Nat D. Williams, and Withers found himself directly connected to this watershed event.

WDIA quickly became the focal point for the city's black entertainment and news. "It was on in everybody's kitchen," Withers recalls: "the voice of the African-American people," and its influence throughout the city was, in his estimation, "somewhat equal to or even greater than the NAACP." The photographer took publicity shots of the DJs who followed Nat Dee, including Dwight "Gatemouth" Moore and Martha Jean "the Queen" Steinberg. When the station started an annual fund-raising show, the Goodwill Revue, Withers covered it and the young WDIA personality, Rufus Thomas, who often cohosted with Nat Dee. Thomas was a graduate of the Rabbit Foot Minstrels, and his broad, burlesque styling would eventually surface in his R & B hits, "The Dog" and "Do the Funky Chicken." Withers shows us Rufus and Nat Dee locked in vaudevillian combat: the kind of funky, down-home outrageousness that helped turn the Goodwill Revue into one of the city's premier black cultural events.

Withers also documented the emergence of the young WDIA DJ, Riley "B. B." King. Withers's photographs may well form the single most comprehensive record we have of the blues great: from the scrawny youth posing with his gospel songbook to the senior citizen performing at his own club. And they bring us news we might not have otherwise heard. When King arrived in the city from Indianola, Mississippi, he's described himself as being, "Well, a little bit, well not actually ashamed. But I was almost afraid to say that I was a blues singer." That kind of music, after all, was "country," especially compared to the glamorous dance bands that King discovered in Memphis. So, King studied Duke Ellington and his great vocalist, Al Hibbler, jazz guitarist Charlie Christian as well as T-Bone Walker. And when it came time to make his first recordings, B.B. brought in some of the city's finest musicians: the Beale Streeters, an in-house band that Withers shows us at the WDIA studio, drummer Phineas Newborn, Sr., whose Family Showband delighted crowds at the Plantation Inn, and bass player Ernest "Tuff" Green who led the hot dance band over at Sunbeam Mitchell's hotel. Then, when King had his first hit—a 1952 cover of Lowell Fulson's "Three O'Clock Blues"—he began touring the black "chitlin' circuit" with the horn-heavy Bill Harvey band. Withers documents Harvey and his dynamite woman

saxophonist, Evelyn Young, flanking an ecstatic King (whose idea of elegance at the time apparently included Bermuda shorts).

The image may surprise us, but to Withers this mixture of country blues and urban dance band was just part of the news in what he calls "a separate America." King, like his contemporaries Percy Mayfield and Ray Charles (then a vocalist with Fulson's band) were tying into a horn and rhythm tradition that went way back. "The big times on Beale Street," the photographer points out, "came, really, in the early days of Jimmy Lunceford, which was before my time." Lunceford, a graduate of Fisk University, came to Memphis in 1926 and went to work at Manassas High School. From that base, he created the Chickasaw Syncopators, a big band so sharp and innovative that it soon moved to the Cotton Club in New York City. There, Lunceford's elegant arrangements and his sense of style—immaculate band uniforms, a long white baton—set an example for the likes of Ellington, Basie, and Tommy Dorsey.

If we look at Withers's portrait of the Tuff Green band, we can see what became of this legacy. By the early 1950s, when Withers returned to being a photographer full-time, the stunning big band machines were no longer economically viable. In their place came smaller six- and eight-piece jump bands that made up for what they lacked in firepower with accuracy, sharpening and emphasizing the beat. Louis Jordan would come into town with his wild stage show, and Beale Street would dance to hits such as "Saturday Night Fish Fry" and "Is You Is or Is You Ain't My Baby?" But Memphis, with its Jimmy Lunceford legacy, taught as much as it learned. We find clues to that in the backstage portrait of Lionel Hampton and a dapper-looking Withers, seen over a piano top littered with sheet music and electric guitars. To Withers's right is fellow black Memphis photographer, Charlie Hooks, but it's the man in the dark slouch hat who turns out to be a key figure.

"That's Professor Lucky Sharpe," says Withers, "the principal of Douglas High. . . . The better bands, the better musicians, came out of Douglas High School." Professor Sharpe hired one of Lunceford's musicians, Dickie Hopson, who trained the Douglas Swingsters, which included first-rate players such as saxophonists Ben Branch and Fred Ford. Not to be outdone, the other black high schools—Manassas and Booker T. Washington—shared band instructor Professor W. T. McDaniels. McDaniels, says Withers, "never got much credit in the annals of history," but this collection of photographs begins to rectify

that. Withers's portrait of the McDaniels-trained Rhythm Bombers documents, in the photographer's estimation, "the beginning of downtown music." Out of the Bombers came B. B. King's saxophonist, Evelyn Young, jazz great Phineas Newborn, Jr., and Frank Strozier and George Coleman, whose hard bop playing would eventually lead them to gigs with Miles Davis, among others. To Withers, this was an important part of what was happening in the 1950s in Memphis: "the growing level of training of musicians and band players. Those were the seeds of yesterday," he goes on to say, "that developed into today."

As we begin to trace the shared influences and recurring themes in Withers's photographs, we have to question the still widely held belief that black music somehow just happened: a spontaneous outpouring of innate talent. These pictures offer clear evidence of how skills got

passed on through the generations—both in the secular and religious fields. The most famous local gospel quartet of the 1950s was The Spirit of Memphis, which used to rehearse, in its early days, over at the house of a fellow parishioner who would soon become Withers's mother-in-law. The exposure that WDIA provided the singers helped convince them to quit their day jobs and become the city's first religious ensemble to go professional. Sponsoring programs that included the Soul Stirrers and their young lead, Sam Cooke, the Pilgrim Travelers with Lou Rawls, and the city's own Southern Wonders, the Spirit of Memphis repeatedly filled the seven-thousand-seat Mason Auditorium. Over at the East Trigg Baptist Church, Reverend Brewster's great singer, Queen C. Anderson, premiered her pastor's compositions, and those, in turn, attracted the field's greatest stars. Cooke covered Brewster's "How Far Am I from Canaan?," Clara Ward and the Ward Singers electrified black churches with "Surely God Is Able," and Mahalia Jackson's version of Brewster's "Move on up a Little Higher" helped establish her as the symbol of gospel music to much of black and white America. Hold up Withers's performance shot of The Spirit of Memphis next to the one of the doo-wop group, The Moonglows, and you can almost hear the influences traveling back and forth.

It was in Memphis, some argue, that these musical styles mixed to form rock and roll. As evidence, they point to Jackie Brenston's "Rocket 88," a record produced by a young pianist named Ike Turner and recorded at a tiny facility in Memphis which would come to be known as Sun Studios. Between 1950 and 1954, Sun's owner, Sam Phillips, seems to have gone down a list of the city's finest black musicians, recording B. B. King, Little Milton, Junior Parker, Rufus Thomas, and Howlin' Wolf, among others. In the light shed by Withers's photographs, we may notice that this list excludes most of the city's brass and reed players. Phillips was looking for something more "primitive" than that sound. What spoke to him were the bone-shaking growls of bluesman Howlin' Wolf, of whom Phillips famously said, "This is where the soul of man never dies." When Junior Parker tried to cut sophisticated Memphis horn arrangements, Phillips directed him toward the rougher blues of "Mystery Train." Even Sun's gospel recordings shied away from harmony and toward shouting.

The strategy resulted in some R & B hits, but Phillips wanted to cross over into the larger white market. At that time, Negroes accounted for 40 percent of the population in Memphis, but black income was less

Pentecostal group, ca. 1954.

11

than half that of whites. What's more, Sun had to compete for those dollars with other independent labels. A light-skinned black Texan named Don Robey took over a little Memphis label called Duke and, between it and his Peacock label, signed up much of the city's talent. In early 1953, when Peacock scored with Big Mama Thornton's "Hound Dog," Phillips had Rufus Thomas record an answer song, "Bear Cat," so similar that Robey sued Sun Records and won.

In 1954, integration still seemed a long way off. The Supreme Court ruled against school segregation in *Brown* v. *Board of Education,* and, of even more importance to Beale Street, Boss Crump died, but Memphis newspapers continued to spell Negro with a small "n." Sam Phillips, for one, was convinced that the only way to reach the mass market with the Memphis sound was to have a white man sing it. In early July of 1954, he had Elvis Presley cut an Arthur "Big Boy" Crudup blues song. White DJ Dewey Phillips broke "That's All Right, Mama" on Memphis radio, and the rest is at least one version of history. From that day on, Phillips switched almost exclusively to recording white performers such as Johnny Cash, Jerry Lee Lewis, and Carl Perkins.

Withers remembers Presley as a "mild-mannered, good-hearted fellow." His photographs show Elvis not so much as the King of Rock and Roll but as a white variant in a continuing black tradition. In Withers's now famous backstage images from WDIA's 1956 and 1957 Goodwill Revues, we see Elvis paying tribute to B. B. King, Rufus Thomas, and Junior Parker, among others. And we get the extraordinary vision of a grinning Presley working his way upstream against a sea of black "Indians." As a teenager, Elvis had not only listened to WDIA but visited Revered Brewster's church for the gospel music and studied Calvin Newborn's dynamic, hip-swiveling stage show. Withers's portraits of Presley reflect these influences while refusing to express any resentment. "He was an unusual escalator," is how Withers puts it. "I don't think he was robbing men. I think he was just learning their styles and their mores by coming around."

We're so used to thinking of rock and roll as a kind of historical climax that it takes a while to see how Withers's work gently but firmly defines it as an adjunct of black culture. His growing journalistic career allowed Withers to place the music in the context of other social

changes. In the summer of 1955, when Presley left Sun to sign with RCA records, Withers had begun to establish a national reputation in the black press for his coverage of the Emmett Till murder/lynching. Two weeks after he made Presley's picture with B. B. King, he documented Rev. Martin Luther King, Jr., and Ralph Abernathy integrating the Montgomery, Alabama, bus system. In Memphis, Withers's partner, mentor, and friend, Negro reporter L. Alex Wilson, supported a white reformist mayor, Edmund Orgill. But when Orgill tried to appoint a black man to a local hospital board, the still-strong remains of the Crump machine stopped him cold. Two years later, Wilson died after a beating he received while he and Withers were covering the integration of the Little Rock, Arkansas, school system.

Many Southern blacks continued to go north in search of freedom. Among local musicians, Junior Parker hit with "Next Time You See Me" and Bobby "Blue" Bland with "Farther Up the Road," but, as Withers puts it, "Memphis has always been a place that drew excitement

Rufus Thomas and **Elvis Presley,** WDIA Goodwill Revue, Ellis Auditorium, December 7, 1956.

< **Evelyn Young, B. B. King, Bill Harvey,** Club Handy, ca. 1951.

to new ideas, but it never stayed hitched on." That had been true as far back as W. C. Handy, who died in 1958. "He had to get into the New York area," says Withers, "to reach his hand out to get his money." So it had been with Jimmy Lunceford. So it was with Phineas Newborn, Jr., and, perhaps most dramatically, with the migration to Chicago by bluesmen like Muddy Waters, Howlin' Wolf, and James Cotton.

Again, Withers brings us this news in a different light. He had documented men like Howlin' Wolf during their first transition out of the cotton fields and into Memphis. Then, in the late 1950s and early 1960s, he records their triumphant return from up north. Many of these bluesmen would soon become legendary idols to rock and rollers, and the history we've received tends to emphasize a kind of blues myth: the lone renegade with his guitar, a social outcast steeped in mystery. That scenario allows for a direct line to adolescent rebellion: Robert Johnson makes his legendary deal with the devil and, voilà—The Rolling Stones. But Withers shows these musicians as part of the larger community. So we see Jimmy Reed playing his rough and tumble blues to a bunch of schoolchildren dressed up in fairy masks. We catch James Cotton trying to keep his jacket uncreased as he takes it from the trunk of his touring car. And we get to witness the baddest of the bad bluesmen congratulating the WDIA Little League team.

It isn't that Withers denies the fierceness of the music. Commenting on his portrait of Howlin' Wolf shouting into the microphone at a Goodwill Revue, the photographer recalls that, "He was so vulgar till they closed the curtain on him." Singing his hit song, "Spoonful," Wolf kept scooping at his crotch with the spoon we see in his right hand. "It was just embarrassing," says Withers, "to all of those families: mothers and fathers and children." But what Withers also helps us see is the calculated necessity behind this stage presence. His portrait of the Howlin' Wolf band in a field off the highway in Brinkley, Arkansas, ranks as one of the single most ferociously ironic and telling images of the urban blues. In dress clothes, hair slicked and cigarettes lit, the band members grin as they mime the backbreaking work of picking cotton. Years before, these men went north to escape this world with all its poverty and cruelty, yet their success depended on making music that evoked it. Withers's shot is a nearly exact visual equivalent, simultaneously celebrating and erasing the past.

For many, the new thing called rock and roll ended when Elvis

entered the army and Buddy Holly's plane went down: "the day the music died." According to this view, popular music took a hiatus until The Beatles arrived a few years later. But the news that these photographs bring is that, in Withers's America, the early 1960s was a time of opportunity. The photographer had already reported B. B. King's switch to a snazzy touring bus. Now, even as he covers sit-ins and voter registration drives, he also celebrates Ray Charles's dazzling soul band. If the airtight horn arrangements on hits such as "What'd I Say" and "Hit the Road, Jack" struck a familiar chord on Beale, it may have had something to do with Ray's bandleader, Hank Crawford, yet another graduate of the Memphis high school music system.

Charles succeeded by mixing gospel with the blues, and Withers chronicles the many religious singers who crossed over around this time. Sam Cooke (who became a friend after the photographer partied with him at the Lorraine Motel) left the Soul Stirrers to lead a powerful soul band. James Brown, Wilson Pickett, Lou Rawls, and Memphis's own O. V. Wright and James Carr, all came out of gospel groups, lured by the chance to make a decent living. Another Memphian, born to a local minister who then moved north, had her first R & B hit in 1960, "Today I Sing the Blues." It wouldn't be until later in the decade that Reverend C. L. Franklin's daughter, Aretha, came back to the South, found the ideal musical settings for her twisting gospel-whooping voice, and became the Queen of Soul.

In the beginning of 1964, The Beatles released "I Want to Hold Your Hand" in the States; their subsequent domination of the charts stifled the careers of many of the very Negro recording stars they admired. The exceptions tended to be in Detroit, with its Motown label, and Memphis. In 1960, Jim Stewart, a white bank teller and sometime country fiddler with the Snearly Ranch Boys, decided to get into the music business. "I had scarcely seen a black," Stewart has said, "till I was grown." But Withers describes him as, "a silent observer of the growth of Elvis Presley [who] saw that it was wise to develop some black music of the same charisma." Stewart ended up in a remodeled movie theater over on East McLemore, where his sister and partner Estelle Paxton ran the record store next door. The two combined their names to form the Stax label.

Stax was a family affair, part of the interconnected community which Withers had already been documenting for decades. It's no

chops playing with club bands led by Willie Mitchell, Gene "Bowlegs" Miller, and Ben Branch. "I knew his daddy," says Withers and then reels off his connections to other members of the Jones family. The MG's' drummer, Al Jackson, Jr., would always be, in Withers's words, "the son of Al Jackson, Sr.," one of the city's most prominent big band leaders. The beat that millions boogied to on Sam and Dave's "Hold On I'm Comin'" worked its way down to the young Jackson through what Withers calls "a legacy of James Crawford, with Jimmy Lunceford, who was the world's greatest drummer." The MG's' original bass player, Lewis Steinberg, was a member of one of the city's most prominent music families. His father had been the piano player at Pee Wee's Saloon on Beale Street, his brother Luther played trumpet with Lionel Hampton, and Lewis worked with Phineas Newborn and Willie Mitchell. Guitarist Steve Cropper—like the bassist Donald "Duck" Dunn who eventually replaced Steinberg—was a young white man who grew up listening to Dewey Phillips and worshipped Mitchell's band as "the pinnacle of cool." These interconnections and shared influences go on and on. "All of us Memphis was not huggin' people," is how Withers puts it, "but we knew of and knew people."

surprise, then, if Withers had, in his words, "both an in and an out" during the golden age of Memphis soul music. Stewart's first hint of success came with Rufus Thomas and his daughter, Carla, singing "Cause I Love You," followed by Carla's own, "Gee Whiz," which went top ten on the pop charts. A lot of the credit for the Memphis sound goes to the Stax house band, Booker T. and the MG's. The group hit with its own funky instrumental, "Green Onions," in 1962, but they also laid down the infectious grooves we associate with Otis Redding, Wilson Pickett, and Sam and Dave, among many others. The MG's—and the modern soul sound they helped define—turn out to be some of Withers's "seeds of tomorrow" that bore fruit.

The group's leader and organ player, Booker T. Jones, graduated from Booker T. Washington High School (as did a slew of other Stax artists including singer William Bell, songwriter David Porter, and Redding's backup band, the Bar-Kays). As a teenager, Jones learned his

The decade and a half of Stax hits that followed would seem to be an exception to the Memphis rule of breeding local players that flower elsewhere. But, as Withers remarks, "It wasn't by the rule; it was by the times. It was just changing times." By the winter of 1960, Memphis had finally integrated its libraries and the zoo, although its downtown stores stayed "whites only" for another two years, and the city's restaurants wouldn't desegregate till halfway through the decade. Even as Bull Connor's fire hoses tried to stop progress in Birmingham, Alabama, Otis Redding's first Stax (and sister label Volt) hit, "These Arms of Mine," was recorded with an integrated band. On the other hand, the Bar-Kays scored with "Last Night" but couldn't tour the South because they consisted of both black and white musicians.

As Stax/Volt continued to produce an amazing number of hits, including Redding's "I've Been Loving You Too Long," and Pickett's "In the Midnight Hour," the mid-1960s uprising in the Los Angeles Watts

Steve Cropper, studio portrait, mid-1960s.

who flew in on his private plane for the funeral, delicately evokes the magnitude of the loss.

Two months later, black garbage workers struck in Memphis, and, after the segregationist mayor refused to negotiate, Withers was there to document the downtown protest that turned into a police riot. On the evening of April 4, 1968, Dr. Martin Luther King, Jr.—in town to help with the strike—stepped out onto the balcony of the Lorraine Motel and was gunned down by an assassin's bullet. As Stax's Booker T. Jones put it, King's death "was the turning point, the turning point for the relations between the races in the South. And it happened in Memphis." Withers not only shows us The Staple Singers paying tribute to the fallen leader but manages to capture the community's sadness in a single, top-heavy image of a teary-eyed Aretha standing before King's widow.

Like other cities across the country, Memphis immediately saw its black neighborhoods go up in smoke. Between the fires and the urban renewal that followed, Beale Street all but disappeared. Remarkably, Stax continued, led by the deep-voiced Manassas High School graduate, Isaac Hayes. "Hayes," Withers notes, "being the star that he was groomed and boomed to be, came out of

region marked a new level of black militancy. That same year, Jim Stewart hired a black PR man, Al Bell (who would eventually rise through the ranks to run the business), and Stax tied itself even more firmly to the Beale Street heritage by signing local blues veterans Albert King and Little Milton. Other Memphis labels were also succeeding. There was Goldwax with James Carr and O. V. Wright, and the Hi recording studio where trumpeter Willie Mitchell was cutting his own instrumental hits.

In 1967, the Memphis recording industry generated an estimated twenty million dollars. The Stax/Volt Revue made a triumphant tour of Europe, playing to wildly enthusiastic fans including members of The Beatles and The Rolling Stones. But with that summer's catastrophic uprisings in Detroit and Newark, racial tensions began to surface within the company. Then, in December 1967, Otis Redding and all but two of the Bar-Kays were killed in a plane crash. Withers's portrait of James Brown,

my immediate neighborhood. He was raised with my cousin's children . . . and he played piano in her house." As a teenager, Hayes sang in two quartets, one gospel and the other modeled on Frankie Lymon's doo-wop sound, and Withers shows us the ambitious young man posing outside WDIA. At Stax, he started as a songwriter, hooking up with another local, David Porter, to compose hits including Sam and Dave's "Soul Man" and Carla Thomas's "B-A-B-Y," among many others.

It was after the traumatic summer of 1968 that Hayes stepped forward as a star in his own right with "Hot Buttered Soul"—Stax's best-selling LP ever—and, later, the Grammy Award-winning "Theme from *Shaft.*" As traced by Withers, his triumph seems almost inevitable, the fruition not only of the horn-rich Memphis sound (Hayes's band leader, Onzie Horn, taught music at Manassas) but of that in-your-face vaudeville styling which had been part of Beale Street for nearly a

Marvin Gaye, Mid-South
Coliseum, late 1970s.

century. Withers documents the outrageousness of the twenty-piece Isaac Hayes Connection in his shots of Hayes and David Porter's niece, Helen Washington. What's more, the photographer's closeness to his subject allows us inside Stax where we get to see the striped riot of Isaac both making fun and taking care of business.

Across town at Hi, Willie Mitchell was cashing in on the skills he'd acquired coming up through the city's dance bands. If, as Withers says, "Tuff Green grew Willie Mitchell," Mitchell now grew his own sound. His and Luther Steinberg's units were the two Memphis bands, Withers points out, "that traveled down through New Orleans, Mississippi, and the edge of Texas and Arkansas." It was in Texas at the end of the 1960s that Mitchell met a young singer named Al Green. The kid had a keening, acrobatic voice that meshed perfectly with Mitchell's lush arrangements. Take a look at Withers's studio portraits of Mitchell as a debonair sideman and, two decades later, Al Green as a street-hungry singer, and you can see the sweet-and-sour mix which led to hits like "Tired of Being Alone," and "I'm Still in Love with You."

Withers's reporting on the music scene becomes less frequent by the late 1970s, and that should bring us its own kind of news. Stax eventually collapsed under both internal and external pressures, Green returned to the church and became the Reverend Al Green, and Beale Street itself was largely reduced to burned-out and abandoned buildings. The age of integration cut both ways. When the blues singer and piano player Memphis Slim returned to his native city in 1978 after decades as an expatriate, he remarked that it was the first time he'd ever been allowed to sit downstairs at the Orpheum Theater. Withers made portraits of the stars who passed through town—Duke Ellington, Dionne Warwick, Dizzy Gillespie—and who were now able to play mainstream venues like the Symphony Auditorium. At the same time, as black music turned into big business, major white newspapers began covering what had been almost exclusively Withers's beat. "Now," says Withers, describing the modern scene, "you got limousines all over America." His most telling image of this change may be his portrait of Marvin Gaye under a ceiling of lights, Memphis cops holding hands to protect a black man, the star so shielded by security we can barely make him out.

Beale Street eventually returned as a tourist attraction, celebrating Memphis greats from W. C. Handy to Elvis Presley. If clubs like Blues Alley with artists such as Ma Rainey II and Little Laura Dukes were mostly nostalgic, at least they kept the memory of the city's music alive. Meanwhile, Withers's career ran a course eerily parallel to those of the musicians he covered. The same way that record label owners would put their names on the music—giving themselves the publishing rights and, therefore, most of the profits—Withers's photographs were often reproduced under another name or no name at all. It's why music fans are likely to recognize his portraits of Elvis or Howlin' Wolf but have no idea who made them, only that they are: "From the collection of . . ." It wasn't until the late 1980s that Withers began to get some of the credit he deserves. He was inducted into the Black Press Hall of Fame, received honorary degrees from the Memphis State University and the Massachusetts College of Art, and, in 2000, the first major retrospective of his photographs began touring nationally.

Even those who know Withers's music photographs are likely to be astonished by the sheer range of his accomplishment, which is presented in this volume for the first time. There are more stories than can possibly be discussed here. Take the role that women play, from influential disc jockey Martha Jean the Queen to Tina Turner (whom we see singing her way out from under her husband Ike's baleful gaze). Or, trace the way Beale Street taught its children, starting with the twins standing on telephone books to reach the WDIA microphone. For another thread, try looking through these images paying attention to the audience reaction. Check out the crowd reaching to erase the barrier between itself and Lionel Hampton. Or the look in the eyes of the GI as he listens to Ruth Brown. Or, for that matter, Danny Thomas trying to answer to a toddler in Handy Park.

Like the music they document, these pictures emerge from inside the community and never leave it too far behind. In the end, that may be the biggest story that Withers brings us. The "good rockin'" these photographs talk about isn't just relaxation music, nor is it simply yesterday's news. Modestly, but with extraordinary clarity and beauty, the photographer manages to document how people build tradition, how they refine and change it, and how they carry it on. Ask Ernest Withers about his accomplishment, and he'll tell you: "I was a photographer. And when you're a photographer, you make a shining light of an image." ∎

"Beale Street in its past great moments."

Rhytmn 'n' Blues Revue, on the midway at the Cottonmaker's Jubilee in the Beale Street Auditorium Park, early 1950s.

W. C. Handy (with trumpet),
The Blues Bowl Parade, inside
Melrose Stadium, ca. 1955.

Opening of the **Al Jackson, Sr.,**
Esso Servicenter, 1963.

> **Bilbo Brown,** "Brown-Skin"
Follies, studio shot, ca. 1949.

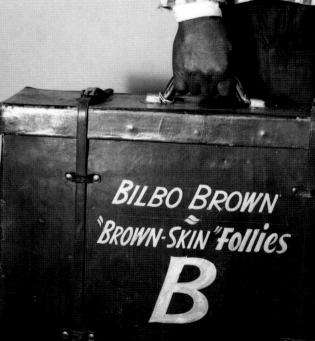

Bones of **Rufus and Bones,**
late 1940s.

"If I could collect those millions of dollars from people that I got artists to pose with! They'd always tell you that they wanted [the pictures], but they never got around to coming and getting them."

Louis Armstrong and fans, The Hippodrome, 1950s.

Pratfall at the Cotton Makers'
Jubilee, 1950s.

Nat D. Williams, *Tri-State Defender* Home Show, early 1950s.

Amateur night at The Palace
Theater, 1940s.

> Twins at WDIA, ca. 1948.

Rufus Thomas and Nat D.
Williams (sitting), WDIA Goodwill
Revue, Mid-South Coliseum,
ca. 1963.

"The Goodwill Revue was the peak
of entertainment. People went to the
Goodwill Revue in the tune of five,
six, or seven thousand."

Dwight "Gatemouth" Moore, ca. 1950.

Overleaf: **Big Maybelle** with **Rufus Thomas** (to her left), 1950s.

The Beale Streeters at WDIA,
ca. 1949.

Dewey Phillips at The Hippodrome, early 1950s.

Clarence "Gatemouth" Brown,
Bill Harvey, Dewey Phillips, W. C.
Handy Theater, ca. 1950.

> **Roy Brown,** unidentified trumpet
player, **Eddie Teamer,** The
Hippodrome, ca. 1951.

Percy Mayfield (with drumsticks)
and band, The Hippodrome, ca.
1951.

Luther Steinberg, early 1950s.

"Lucy Campbell was a great woman and teacher, and her songs are sung in churches all over the country every Sunday....My mother was her seamstress."

Lucy Campbell (at piano) and singers, *Tri-State Defender* Home Show, early 1950s.

Count Basie, Ruth Brown, Billy Eckstine, The Hippodrome, 1950s.

> **Ruth Brown,** The Hippodrome, 1950s.

Reverend W. Herbert Brewster
(standing in rear), **Queen C.
Anderson** (third from right in
profile), **The Reed Singers,** East
Trigg Baptist Church,
ca. 1952.

"Reverend Brewster was a great
orator, a great writer, and a great
producer of music."

(Left) **Helen Humes, Big Joe Turner,** unidentified, lobby of The Palace Theater, 1950s.

(Right) **Helen Humes** onstage at The Palace Theater, 1950s.

Lionel Hampton (with trumpet), backstage at The Hippodrome, mid-1950s. Left to right: **Charlie Hooks, Ernest Withers, Hampton, Professor Lucky Sharpe,** two unidentified people.

Remnants of the **Tuff Green Band,** 1950s.

< **Maurice "Fess" Hulbert, Sr.** (left), and **Al Hibbler,** backstage at the Elks Club, 1950s.

Overleaf: **Tuff Green Band,** Beale Street Auditorium, ca. 1950.

"They were the first real young band that was brought to downtown Memphis. Came mostly from Manassas [High]. Introduced to Sunbeam by Haynes Jones...trained by Professor MacDaniels, and played at Mitchell's."

The Rhythm Bombers, Mitchell Hotel, late 1940s.

> **Louis Jordan** (right) and his father, The Hippodrome, 1950s.

B. B. King tour, Fayette,
Mississippi, 1950s.

< The young **Riley "B. B." King,**
studio portrait, late 1940s.

"Bill Harvey was a great saxophonist, a star in his own right . . . Everybody who came to Memphis would marvel over him. He just didn't have the discipline of others."

Bill Harvey onstage at The Palace
Theater, late 1940s.

Good times with the **Phineas Newborn Family Showband,** Flamingo Room, early 1950s.

**Phineas Newborn Family
Showband,** Flamingo Club,
early 1950s.

**Phineas Newborn Family
Showband** (Phineas with glasses
at the piano), 1950s.

Calvin Newborn (on guitar),
Flamingo Room, 1950s.

"He's in his high school uniform
then, but he's quite an adult now."

Frank Strozier, ca. 1952.

Fred Ford, ca. 1954.

"Ben Branch was a great musician. He was the boy Martin King was talking to when he was assassinated."

Ben Branch (on saxophone), Club Tropicana, 1950s.

The Veltones, mid-1950s.

"I'd like to have that money [Robey] has in his pocket. He had a lot of money—wasn't the credit card days."

Johnny Otis (left) and **Don Robey,**
Sunbeam Mitchell's office,
mid-1950s.

Big Mama Thornton (with maracas) and friends (left to right) **Johnny Ace, Eddie Tamer, B. B. King, Rubysteen Hudson, Bill Harvey, Thornton,** unidentified, Beale Street Auditorium, ca. 1953.

Johnny Ace's car, Hernando Street, ca. 1953.

< **Johnny Ace,** WDIA, early 1950s.

"No, he [re: the audience member in suspenders on far right] don't come off the fields. Not straight to a nightclub on Beale Street. Men got dressed up!"

Lowell Fulson (with guitar), The Hippodrome, mid-1950s.

> B. B. King (left) and Ray Charles, mid-1950s.

Overleaf: B. B. King's tour bus, "Big Red," Beale Street, ca. 1956.

B. B. King (second from left) with **Little Willie John** (to left of King), front entrance to The Hippodrome, ca. 1957.

The Spirit of Memphis, City
Auditorium, early 1960s.

**The New Salem Baptist Church
Choir,** ca. 1950.

"They were highly honored, Pop Staples and them, every time they came."

The Staple Singers, City Auditorium, WDIA Goodwill Revue, mid-1950s.

Women's club, private home,
mid- to late-1950s.

"[Laura Dukes] was even a greater singer than Lillie Mae Glover, but she just wasn't as photogenic."

Little Laura Dukes, with jukebox, Elks Club on Beale Street, early 1950s.

Waitresses with jukebox,
Plantation Inn, West Memphis,
early 1950s.

Junior Parker, studio portrait, mid-
1950s.

Beale Street Fred, studio portrait,
mid-1950s.

WDIA junior king and queen,
mid-1950s.

The Sparrow, mid-1950s.

The Moonglows, WDIA Goodwill
Revue, Ellis Auditorium, December
7, 1956.

"[Elvis] was young and he was not chaperoned by Colonel Parker and them around black people. That was his own hobbyistic style—of coming around African-American people."

Elvis backstage, WDIA Goodwill Revue, Ellis Auditorium, December 7, 1956.

Clockwise from top left: **Brook Benton** and **Elvis Presley; Junior Parker, Elvis Presley, Bobby Blue Bland; Willa Monroe** and **Elvis Presley,** WDIA Goodwill Revue, Ellis Auditorium, December 6, 1957.

< **Elvis Presley** and **B. B. King,** WDIA Goodwill Revue, Ellis Auditorium, December 7, 1956.

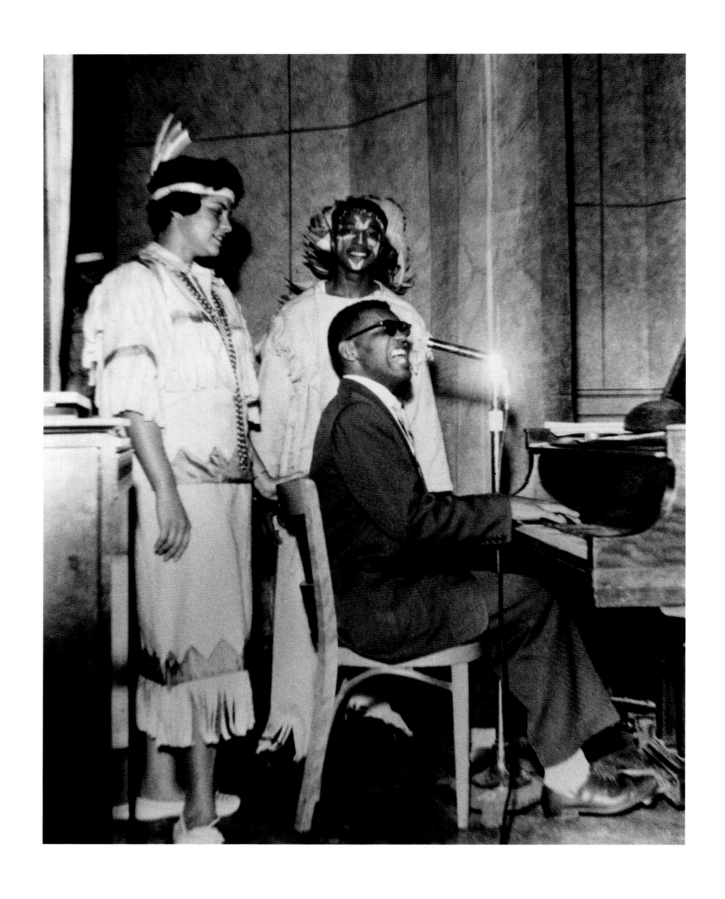

Ray Charles, WDIA Goodwill
Revue, Ellis Auditorium, December
7, 1956.

Roscoe Gordon and **Sam Phillips,**
Sun Studios, 1956.

Rubysteen Hudson (seated) and
Little Esther Phillips, WHHM
studio, ca. 1957.

Erskine Hawkins, Roy Hamilton
(with white flower), **Clifford Miller**
and wife, Flamingo Club, late
1950s.

Snearly Ranch Boys, Cotton Club,
West Memphis, late 1950s.

Evelyn Young with **B. B. King** band, Club Handy, late 1950s.

Clara Ward Singers, Clayborn Temple, ca. 1958.

"This was at Union Station as they came out of the segregated side and had the press conference in the parking lot. But still freedom!"

Marian Anderson (third from left),
Union Station, early 1950s.

Nick Adams and **Elvis Presley**
flanked by the **Lansky Brothers,**
ca. 1958.

Frankie Lymon (center) with **Little Willie Dunn** and fan, ca. 1958.

Bobby Blue Bland (center) and
band, Club Handy, late 1950s.

> Bass player, **Bobby Blue Bland**
band, Club Handy, late 1950s.

Brook Benton (center), late 1950s.

Homer Banks (on bass) and
Robert Honeymoon Garner,
Flamingo Club, 1959.

Overleaf: **Club Ebony,** early 1960s.

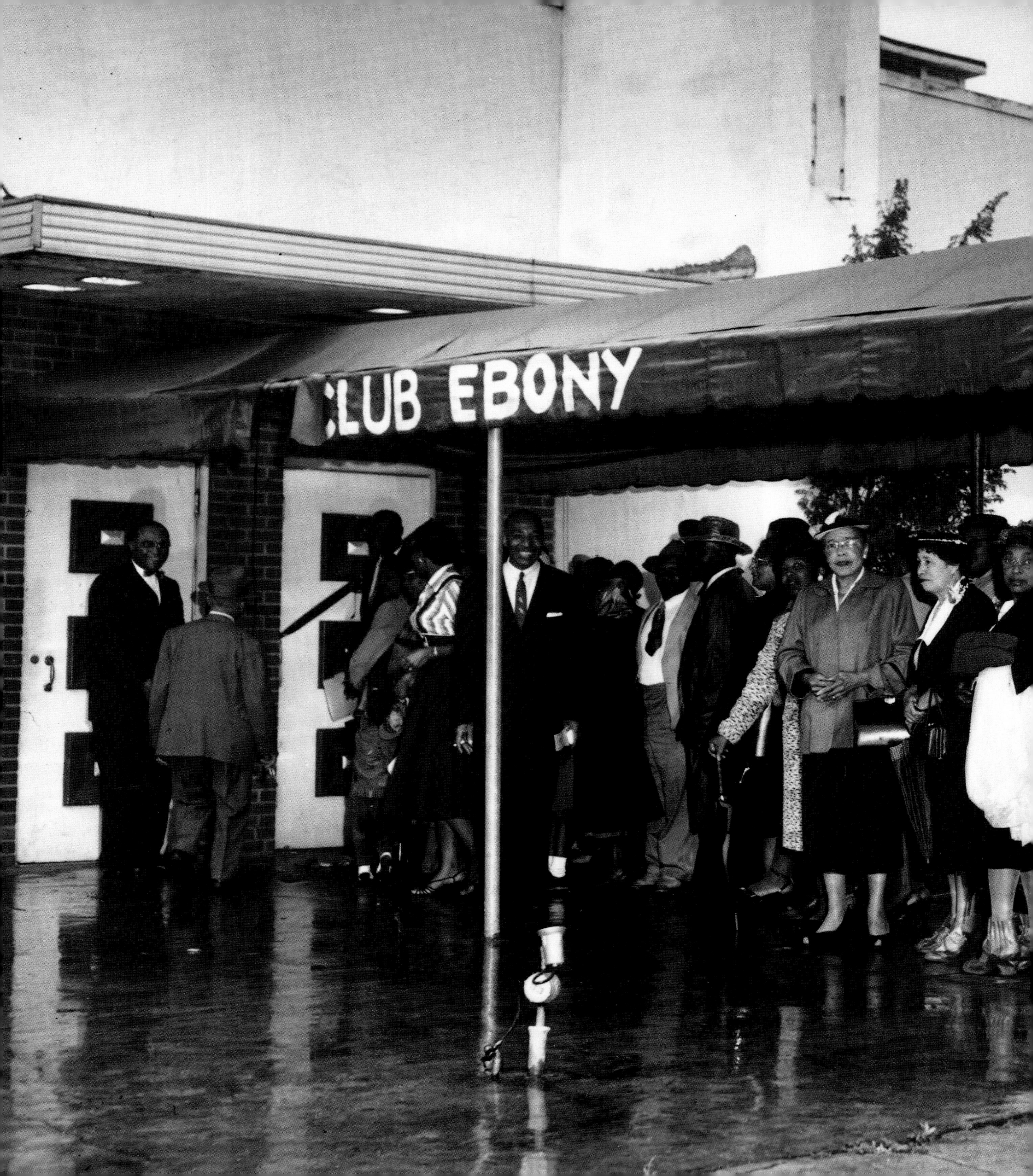
CLUB EBONY

Ray Charles and **Hank Crawford,**
City Auditorium, ca. 1961.

Jay and the Twilighters,
Plantation Inn, West Memphis,
c. 1962.

Jimmy Reed, WDIA Goodwill
Revue, City Auditorium, ca. 1961.

> **Howlin' Wolf,** Memphis grocery
store, ca. 1951.

Howlin' Wolf, WDIA Goodwill
Revue, City Auditorium, ca. 1960.

Bluesmen (left to right:
unidentified, **B. B. King, Howlin'
Wolf, Muddy Waters, Ivory Joe
Hunter** and WDIA Little Leaguers,
City Auditorium, ca. 1960.

Little Walter (left) and **James
Cotton,** ca. 1961.

Howlin' Wolf Band, Brinkley,
Arkansas, ca. 1961.

Albert King, Club Paradise, early
1960s.

Junior Parker with **Bobby Blue Bland Band,** Club Handy, 1960s.

**L. C. Bates, Aretha Franklin, Sam
Cooke,** Lorraine Motel, 1961.

Ike and **Tina Turner,** Club
Paradise, ca. 1962.

Tina Turner and an **Ikette,** Club
Paradise, ca. 1962.

"Oh, Carla Thomas is a great image. She was as beautiful as she could be."

Carla Thomas, mid-1960s.

Solomon Burke, Ellis Auditorium,
WDIA Goodwill Revue, ca. 1962.

<∧ **James Brown,** Mid-South
Coliseum, ca. 1965.

O. V. Wright, studio portrait
ca. 1964.

> **James Carr,** studio portrait,
mid-1960s.

Mahalia Jackson, WDIA tribute to
W. C. Handy, Crump Stadium, mid-
1960s.

Aretha Franklin, Club Paradise,
November 26, 1966.

Sam Cooke's wake, Chicago,
December 17, 1964.

"That was just a little comin'-up group that had a studio sitting."

Unidentified girl group, studio portrait, 1960s.

Sam the Sham (left), and **Rufus Thomas,** Mid-South Coliseum, ca. 1966.

Lloyd Price (third from left) and friends, The Palace Theater, 1960s.

"Booker T. was a younger boy, younger than the peer group he was with. A young, ingenious musician."

Booker T. Jones, studio portrait, mid-1960s.

James Brown (seated) arriving for Otis Redding's funeral, Memphis Airport, December 1967.

< **Otis Redding** and the **Bar-Kays,** studio portrait, mid-1960s.

Staple Singers, at the spot Martin
Luther King, Jr., was killed,
Lorraine Motel, 1968.

Aretha Franklin with **Coretta Scott King,** SCLC Convention, Club Paradise, July 1968.

Re-formed **Bar-Kays,** WLOK
studio, December 1978.

Johnny Taylor, Stax mailroom,
February 1969.

Jerry Butler (seated), Stax
Studios, ca. 1969.

Little Milton, B. B. King, Albert King, Club Paradise, early 1970s.

"This was a big day in Mississippi honoring Charles Evers [mayor of Fayette, brother of Medgar Evers]."

Reverend Cleophus Robinson, Fayette, Mississippi, 1969.

< **Diana Ross,** Fayette, Mississippi, 1969.

"They were coming to be, coming to be."

Isaac Hayes (far left) at the Big
Star Show, outside WDIA, ca.
1958.

David Porter in the Stax parking
lot, ca. 1970.

Isaac Hayes, Club Paradise, ca. 1972.

> **Helen Washington,** Club Paradise, ca. 1972.

**John Smith, Rufus Thomas, Bill
Russell,** in the Stax parking lot,
April 1971.

"Be good to me, baby."

Luther Ingram, unidentified, at
Stax, ca. 1972.

Al Green, studio portrait,
ca. 1970.

> **Willie Mitchell,** studio portrait,
early 1950s.

"**Al Green** was commemorated by the city. They did a commemorative to him and his mother. Had an **Al Green Day** at the Coliseum."

Al Green, Mid-South Coliseum,
August 1973.

Willie Mitchell Band, ca. 1960s.

Psychedelic pair, ca. 1970s.

Jim Stewart, of Stax Records,
Memphis Music Awards, ca. 1972.

"Free Angela Davis," rally outside
City Hall, ca. 1971.

**William Bell, Al Bell, Billy
Eckstine,** Stax Studios, 1970s.

Stax in ruins, East McLemore, late 1970s.

Ray Charles with black and white fans, mid-1970s.

< **Moms Mabley,** Mid-South Coliseum, 1970s.

The Raeletts of the Ray Charles
band, Club Paradise, 1972.

Duke Ellington with the Memphis Symphony, City Auditorium, July 1970.

Count Basie, City Auditorium,
1970s.

Dizzy Gillespie (center), Mid-South Coliseum, 1970s.

Joe Simon, Mid-South Coliseum,
1970s.

"This was at a little restaurant. This guy was a doctor—who was enthused."

Charley Pride, Memphis restaurant, 1970s.

Dionne Warwick, Memphis Music
Awards, June 1972.

Midget singer, Club Paradise,
1960s.

"Lillie Mae Glover, her greatest days was her last days, in that she took on the Ma Rainey title."

Ma Rainey II, studio portrait, 1970s.

> **Big Ella,** Club Paradise, 1960s

Roberta Flack, Mid-South
Coliseum, mid-1970s.

Previous page: **Jerry Lee Lewis,**
B. B. King, Charlie Rich, Holiday
Inn, Rivermont, Tennessee, 1980s.

Danny Thomas (with trumpet) and the **mayor of Beale Street** (with cane), Handy Park, early 1960s.

Memphis Slim, Peabody Hotel, ca.
1978.

> **B. B. King,** the B. B. King Club,
Beale Street, 1994.

Frontis

"Isaac was very fond of me, for some reason. I lost a boy in 1974. My son [Wendell] got hit by an automobile and stayed in a coma. Isaac paid the air ambulance and lifted my wife, my son and I out of the hospital there at Huntington Beach, California, to the airport and then to the Memphis hospital."

p 6

Hampton, a multiinstrumentalist, was best known as a vibraphone player. Born in 1908, he played with almost every jazz great of his era, including Louis Armstrong and Benny Goodman. His "Flyin' Home" in 1942 and subsequent hits were precursors of R & B, and his own big band featured many jazz greats, including Dinah Washington, Dexter Gordon, and Charles Mingus.

p 8

Rev. Franklin, who died in 1984, was born Clarence LeVaughn Franklin in Sunflower County, Mississippi, in 1915. After pastoring in Memphis, he moved north and settled in at the New Bethel Baptist Church in Detroit. There, he became the most famous preacher on the gospel circuit with more than seventy-five recorded songs and sermons, including "How the Eagle Stirreth Her Nest."

"[Reverend Franklin] had New

Salem Church on South 4th Street, around the corner from Lucy Street where Aretha was born."

p 11

Memphis is the world headquarters of the Church of God in Christ (COGIC), founded in 1907 by Bishop C. H. Mason and now the second largest pentecostal group in America.

"All of them were great voices at that time. A pentecostal Church of God in Christ group with Mattie Flag Porter [second from left], headed by Mattie Wigley [third from left] and Deborah Mason Patterson [at piano], Bishop Mason's daughter."

p 12

"Bill Harvey was special, not only because of his skill, but his personality. He'd raise my spirits. If I was feeling bad about not being as good as T-Bone or Charlie Christian, Bill would remind me that we're all unique. . . . Bill played a band like Willie Mays played the outfield. He had it covered."
—B. B. King

p 13

Rufus appeared at this Goodwill Revue as "Rocking Horse," the Indian responsible for bringing rock and roll into the "tribe."

p 15

Cropper was the guitarist for Booker T. and the MG's. He was born in Missouri in 1941 and moved to Memphis in 1950. Among his many other hit compositions, he cowrote "In the Midnight Hour" and "(Sittin' on) the Dock of the Bay."

"When I came to Memphis and finally had my own radio, I used to listen to WDIA and at midnight they would play gospel music. That really turned me around."
—Steve Cropper

p 16

Gaye, born in 1939, sang with the Moonglows before recording a long string of Motown hits, including "Pride and Joy" (1963), "I Heard It Through the Grapevine" (1968), "Let's Get It On" (1973). In 1984, he was shot to death by his father, a preacher.

p 18

"Rhytmn 'n' Blues Revue," on the midway at the Cottonmaker's Jubilee in the Beale Street Auditorium Park, early 1950s.

"Beale Street in its past great moments."

p 19

(Left to right, standing): National Grand Organizer Jones of the Improved

Benevolent Protective Order of the Elks (I.B.P.O.E.); Lieutenant George W. Lee, organizer of the Blues Bowl and member of Bluff City 96 Elks; Handy. W. C. Handy, born in Florence, Alabama, in 1873, was the son of slaves. A cornet player, he got his early experience with minstrel shows, moving to Memphis in 1905. Handy wrote "Mister Crump Blues" (later "The Memphis Blues") in 1909. After composing other hits, including "The St. Louis Blues" and starting his own orchestra, he moved to Chicago in 1918, then to New York City. Blind in his later years, he died in 1958.

"Walking in the footprints of W. C. Handy, Lieutenant Lee was a strong get-it-done guy and promoter."

p 20

(Left to right): "Little" Laura Dukes, a Beale Street singer and the daughter of Alex Dukes, W. C. Handy's drummer; unidentified single-string bass player from the Beale Street jug band; Son Jess, a blind trumpet player formerly with W. C. Handy's band; Hank O'Day, a legendary sax player with the Al Jackson, Sr., band; unidentified.

"These were the top people."

p 21

Bilbo Brown, "Brown-Skin" Follies, studio shot, ca. 1949.

"The Palace Theater had a collection of these vaudeville shows …from a minstrel act to shake dancers and Cinderella dancers. Bilbo Brown was a creator of shows, but Bilbo Brown's 'Brown-Skin' Follies never really grew as big as his projection."

Note: Unless otherwise indicated, all pictures are set in Memphis and all quotes are by Ernest C. Withers.

p 22

Robert Couch was the "Bones" part of the Beale Street comedy team Rufus and Bones. They appeared in the first film ever shot in Memphis, the all-black musical *Halleluja,* made in 1929. In the late forties, when Al Jackson, Sr., led the house band at the Palace Theater, the comedy team was a regular warm-up act.

"They were kind of a black Dean Martin and Jerry Lewis, with Rufus doing the straight lines and Bones doing all kinds of crazy things."
—Memphis musician Herman Green

p 23

Armstrong, the great jazz trumpeter, singer and arranger, was born in 1901 in New Orleans and died in 1971.

"If I could collect those millions of dollars from people that I got artists to pose with! They'd always tell you that they wanted [the pictures], but they never got around to coming and getting them."

p 24

The Cotton Makers' Jubilee was founded in 1934 as an alternative to the all-white Memphis Cotton Carnival on Main Street. It soon grew to be larger and more popular than the white event and incorporated talent shows and a Cotton Carnival king and queen.

"The Cotton Jubilee is the biggest thing that ever happened in Memphis with Negroes."

p 25

Williams, born in 1907, was a teacher at Booker T. Washington High School, the author of a weekly column, "Down on Beale," for Negro papers, and served as the city editor of the Memphis *Tri-State Defender*. As well as an all-round promoter of Beale Street and black culture, "Nat Dee" became the first Negro disc jockey when WDIA went to all-black programming in 1948. He died in 1983.

"Nat D. Williams was my basic trainer. He was a man that was in tune with what went on."

p 27

WDIA became the first radio station to go to all-black programming in 1948.

"Bert Ferguson was the founder and owner of WDIA: a country-western radio station, and it wasn't going anywhere. It was suggested he needed to go and bend to a Negro audience. And he so did."

p 28

Thomas was born in Cayce, Mississippi, in 1917, attended the Booker T. Washington High School in Memphis, traveled with the Rabbit Foot Minstrels as a tap dancer, and joined WDIA as a DJ in his early thirties. He recorded for Sun Records and emceed both the Goodwill Revues and amateur nights at the Palace Theater.

"I would put together everything that I shot. In advance. Then their [WDIA's] management people

decided what they wanted….The Goodwill Revue was the peak of entertainment. People went to the Goodwill Revue in the tune of five, six, or seven thousand."

p 29

Moore, born in 1913, began as a blues singer with the Rabbit Foot Minstrels and had a hit with the soulful "Did You Ever Love a Woman?" in the 1940s. In 1949, he had a sudden conversion to gospel music in the middle of a night-club performance. Moore hosted WDIA's afternoon "Jesus Is the Light of the World."

"Gatemouth Moore is a legend of Beale Street equal to, parallel, or trained by Nat Williams…and a picture hound!"

pp 30–31: Big Maybelle was born Maybelle Lois Smith in Jackson, Tennessee, in 1924. She won a prize in an amateur singing competition in Memphis in 1932 and went on to become a bluesy, jook-joint singer, with hits like "Gabbin Blues" in 1953. Big Maybelle died in relative obscurity in 1971.

p 32

(Left to right): Earl Forrest on drums, Billy Duncan on sax, Bobby "Blue" Bland standing in rear, Johnny Ace at the piano. The Beale Streeters were an in-house band at WDIA. Its members all went on to be Beale Street stars, and all except Bland appeared on B. B. King's first hit, "Three O'Clock Blues."

p 33

Phillips, born in 1926, began DJing his "Red, Hot & Blue" show on WHBQ in October 1949. In response to and in competition with Negro programming, Phillips featured wild, stream-of-consciousness patter and the hottest music around. He died in 1968.

"If a white kid listened to WDIA in his home, his mother might get quite upset. They were afraid to listen to it. But [white] people like Dewey Phillips were legitimate."
—Dr. David Evans, Memphis State University

"Dewey was not white. Dewey *had* no color." —Rufus Thomas

p 34

Gatemouth Brown was born in 1924 and began as a drummer for the Brown Skin Models. It was his guitar playing and his singing, however, that drew the attention of Houston promoter Don Robey, who started his Peacock label in 1949 to put out Brown's records. His hits include 1954's "Okie Dokie Blues." Brown still tours the blues circuit.

p 35

Born in 1925, singer Roy Brown wrote and recorded one of the proto-rock and roll songs, "Good Rockin' Tonight," in 1947. Other hits included "Hard Luck Blues" from 1950. He died in 1981. Teamer was a DJ at WHHM in competition with the likes of Dewey Phillips and WDIA's "Hot Rod" Hulbert.

"This was in that first round of DJs in Memphis. 'The Howlin' Screamin' Teema-Leema!' He was a raving type."

p 36, top

Mayfield, born in 1920, was known as the Poet of the Blues. He wrote and recorded the hit "Please Send Me Someone to Love" for the Specialty label in 1950. His performing career was halted by a near-fatal car wreck in 1952, but he then became a songwriter for Ray Charles, contributing "Hit the Road, Jack," among others. He died in 1984.

"In the R and B field, we all took note when Percy Mayfield rolled into Memphis with his name written all over the side of a long bus. That said prestige and permanence." —B. B. King

p 36, bottom

Steinberg, a member of one of Beale Street's most important musical families, was a trumpeter with Lionel Hampton. His father played piano on Beale; his brother, Lewis, was the original bass player with Booker T. and the MG's; and his wife was WDIA personality Martha Jean Steinberg.

"Music in Memphis arrived with Willie Mitchell and Luther Steinberg."

p 37

Campbell was not only the first black woman composer to publish a gospel song ("Something Within" in 1919) but also went on to be one of the genre's

most important writers. Born in Mississippi in 1885, she lived in Memphis from 1889 until her death in 1962. Campbell became a teacher at Booker T. Washington High School in 1911. Her compositions include "He Understands, He'll Say 'Well Done'" and "In the Upper Room."

"Woman, we are somebody— clothed in the sun. No need for costume jewelry or real diamonds, rubies or pearls. The sun is enough." —Lucy Campbell

"Lucy Campbell was a great woman and teacher, and her songs are sung in churches all over the country every Sunday. . . . My mother was her seamstress."

p 38

Basie and vocalist Eckstine both led legendary big bands. Brown, born Ruth Weston in 1928, had her first hit in 1949, "So Long." A great early R & B singer, she followed with "5-10-15 Hours" in 1952 and others, including "Mama, He Treats Your Daughter Mean" in 1953.

"Once when I went south with Billy Eckstine, George Shearing and Count Basie, I had to repeat 'Mama, He Treats Your Daughter Mean' eight times in a row before I was able to leave the stage." —Ruth Brown

p 39

Brown became known as Miss Rhythm.
"They built a skating rink known as The Hippodrome. And as it began to dwindle and not draw, they thought that it would make more money by turning it into a nightclub for big bands [in the late 1940s]."

p 40

In the 1950s, Reverend Brewster, the legendary gospel composer, broadcast live on the radio over WDIA and WHBQ. He was born just east of Memphis around 1897, was called to preach at age sixteen, and came to Memphis in 1924.

"[Queen C. Anderson] had the most beautiful voice you ever heard. She could make a high voice, and with her low soprano, she would louden it and widen it and deepen it. It was just amazing to anybody that heard it." —Reverend Brewster

"Reverend Brewster was a great orator, a great writer, and a great producer of music."

p 41, left

Humes, born in 1913, replaced Billie Holiday in the Count Basie Band in 1938 and emerged as one of the leading women jazz singers of the 1940s. Turner was born in 1911 and died in 1985. Out of Kansas City, he began as a gospel and street-corner singer, became known as a boogie-woogie blues shouter, and helped bring in the R & B era with his fifties hits, including "Flip, Flop and Fly" and "Shake, Rattle and Roll" (the latter covered by Bill Haley and the Comets).

p 41, right

Among Humes's hit singles were "Be-

ba-ba-le-ba" and "Million Dollar Secret." She first recorded as a teenager and joined the Count Basie Band because record producer John Hammond snuck her into an amateur night competition at Harlem's Apollo Theater. She died in 1981.

p 42

Hulbert may be best known as the father of WDIA (and then Baltimore) DJ Maurice "Hot Rod" Hulbert, but he was a club owner, entrepreneur and Beale Street personality in his own right. Among other innovations, he started the first black dance academy in Memphis in the 1920s. According to Withers, Hulbert was "Mr. Beale Street himself, second only to Nat Williams." Hibbler, the great ballad singer, was born blind in Tyro, Mississippi, in 1915. He got his start by winning a talent contest in Memphis, then went on to sing with the Jay McShann Band and Duke Ellington's orchestra. Among the baritone's many hits was "Unchained Melody" in 1955. Hibbler was a prominent supporter of the early civil rights movement and often marched with Dr. King.

p 43, top

(Left to right): Photographer Charlie Hooks, brother of Benjamin Hooks, a well-known Memphis attorney, preacher and civil rights activist; Ernest C. Withers; Hampton; Professor Lucky Sharpe, the principal of Douglas High School; unidentified.

"We had our cameras, and I would have said, 'Take my picture.' We were just talking."

p 43, bottom

Squash Campbell (third from left), Lewis Steinberg (fifth from left, rear), Sunny Shannon on trumpet.

"[Sunny] came out of that Rhythm Bombers area, out of Manassas [High School]. Tuff Green was a total generation ahead of these kids."

pp 44–45: (Left to right): Sunny Shannon (piano), unidentified (sax), Richard "Tuff" Green (bass), Billy Taylor (vocal), Bubba Chin (sax), Mr. Howard (drums), Fat Sunny (sax), Matt Garrett (trumpet, teacher at Manassas High).

"I always tell people that the original rock and roll band was Tuff Green in Memphis. Tuff Green and his Rocketeers. I used to go to the Mitchell Hotel, man, they used to sneak me in there, '47, '48."
—Jazz great Moses Allison

p 46

(Standing left to right): Reamus Mac-Phee (drummer), unidentified piano and horn player, Eddie Smith (horn; later professor of music at the University of Michigan), Sunbeam Mitchell, Haynes Jones; (sitting, left to right): unidentified, Evelyn Young, Emerson Able (later bandmaster at Manassas and with Isaac Hayes), Cleophus Johnson (later bandmaster at Morehouse University), Calvin Kincaid.

"They were the first real young band that was brought to downtown Memphis. Came mostly from Manassas [High]. Introduced to Sunbeam by Haynes Jones…trained by Professor MacDaniels, and played at Mitchell's."

p 47

Jordan, born in 1908 in Brinkley, Arkansas, dominated the R & B charts in the 1940s. Eleven of his humorous, driving singles were on the Harlem Hit Parade in 1946 alone. Too often overlooked as a mere novelty act, Jordan was an influential jump-band leader and performer who died in 1975.

"My father taught me music."
—Louis Jordan

"He was out of New Orleans as an entertainer, but his hometown was Brinkley because he was raised with my daddy's people."

p 49

Born Riley King in Indianola, Mississippi in 1925, the blues singer was nicknamed B.B. (for "Blues Boy") after he came to Memphis, ca. 1946.

"He was a raw guy. In fact, B.B. is one of the most unusual men that I ever met in my life….Maybe the greatest unwritten story on B. B. King was that B.B. was not literate when he went into the music business. He hired a guy named Cups, and he learned [to read], plus keeping his head."

p 50

"Even though Bill Harvey was a fabulous musician . . . drinking muddied his mind and made him sick." —B. B. King

"Bill Harvey was a great saxophonist, a star in his own right … Everybody who came to Memphis would marvel over him. He just didn't have the discipline of others."

p 51

The Phineas Newborn Family Showband is in the background with Phineas Newborn, Sr., on drums. Father of noted Memphis musicians, Newborn Sr. played the Midnight Rambles at the Palace Theater in the 1930s, toured with Lionel Hampton, backed Gatemouth Moore and Tuff Green among many others, and was on B. B. King's first records. (Seated left to right): Homer Banks (musician), Wanda Jones (trombonist and wife-to-be of Calvin Newborn), unidentified, Beale Street Britt (comedian).

p 52

The Flamingo Club was upstairs at Hernando and Beale Streets, formerly the Hotel Men's Improvement Club. Newborn's band briefly left the club to tour with Ike Turner and Jackie Brenston behind what many consider the first rock and roll record, "Rocket 88."

p 53

(Left to right): Harold Mabon, Frank Strozier (partly hidden), Phineas Newborn, Sr. (drums), Calvin Newborn (trombone), Phineas Newborn, Jr. (piano), unidentified, Tuff Green. Phineas Newborn, Jr., was born in 1931

and died in 1989. A child prodigy, he played in Memphis high school bands and was soon stunning visiting jazz players with his virtuosity. Newborn opened at Carnegie Hall in 1957, recorded on the Atlantic label, and went on to tour with Count Basie's Band, Sarah Vaughan, and Lester Young, among others. He spent the end of his life living with his mother, back in Memphis, and going in and out of mental institutions.

"He was a genius who could play Chopin and Mozart when he was only a child. Folks were calling him the new Art Tatum."
—B. B. King

p 54

Frank Strozier on sax. Born in 1933, Calvin Newborn was a guitar showman and a multiinstrumentalist. He played with his father's band and recorded with his brother, Phineas Jr., as well as other jazz players such as Earl Hines. B. B. King helped him pick out his first guitar at Nathan's pawn shop on Beale Street, and Elvis Presley used to come to watch his wild stage show.

"[At the Flamingo Room] you'd have guitar players to come in and battle me, like Pee Wee Crayton and Gatemouth Brown, and I was battlin' out there, tearin' they behind up, 'cause I was dancin', playin', puttin' on a show, slidin' across the floor…."
—Calvin Newborn

p 55

Strozier graduated from high school in Memphis (where he was born in 1937), then moved to Chicago in 1954. He eventually played be-bop sax with Miles Davis, among many others.

"He's in his high school uniform then, but he's quite an adult now.

Frank Strozier was a great saxo-phonist, and he rose to national popularity. His father was a pharmacist. He was from the early Rhythm Bombers, a little younger than Phineas Newborn. He played on my ball team when I was on the police force."

p 56

Born in 1930, Fred Ford was a prominent Beale Street sax player. He toured with Bill Harvey and the Harlem to Havana Revue as a teenager, recorded with Phineas Newborn, Jr., was in the early B. B. King band, and is the man who barks at the end of Big Mama Thornton's hit single "Hound Dog." Ford died in 1999.

"After playing across the river in Arkansas, I'd hurry back to Beale Street on a Saturday night just to hear Fred Ford jam." —B. B. King

p 57

Branch, trained by Dickie Hopson in the Douglas Swingsters, had the house band at Johnny Curry's Club Tropicana in north Memphis. His band members would include Booker T. Jones, Duck Dunn, and Lewis Steinberg, all eventually of Booker T. and the MG's. Memphis's premier vocal group of the time, the Veltones, sang with his band, and Branch also gave Isaac Hayes his first professional job as a singer. Branch was at the Lorraine Motel with Dr. Martin Luther King, Jr., on April 4, 1968.

"Ben Branch was a great musician. He was the boy Martin King was talking to when he was assassinated."

p 58

Memphis's hottest vocal group of the fifties, the Veltones was the first black group recorded by Jim Stewart on what would be Stax Records. They sang back-up on Carla Thomas's hit "Gee Whiz."

p 59

Otis, born Johnny Veliotes in 1921, was a mainstay of Los Angeles R & B. After he hit with "Double Crossing Blues" in 1949, he signed with Robey's Peacock label in 1953. That same year, his band backed Big Mama Thornton on "Hound Dog," and in 1958 he came back with his own hit, "Willie and the Hand Jive." Otis also acted as a talent scout for Robey. Robey, born in 1903, died in 1975. One of the leading independent record executives of the 1950s, he recorded many Memphis musicians on his Peacock label and inherited others by taking over Duke Records from WDIA's David J. Mattis and Bill Fitzgerald. A light-skinned Negro, Robey was as notorious as his white counterparts for underpaying his musicians.

"Johnny Otis was a creator of shows, and Don Robey was a record producer and businessman. I'd like to have that money [Robey] has in his pocket. He had a lot of money—wasn't the credit card days."

p 60

Born John Marshall Alexander in 1929, Ace died tragically in 1954. He played piano on B. B. King's first recordings,

then signed with Robey's Duke Records in 1952. Ace's brief career included the hits "My Song" and "Pledging My Love."

p 61, top

(Left to right): Johnny Ace, Eddie Teamer, B. B. King, WLOK disc jockey Rubysteen Hudson, Bill Harvey, Thornton, unidentified. Born Willie Mae Thornton in 1926, Big Mama toured as a teenager with the Hot Harlem Revue, signed to Peacock Records in 1951, and released her major hit (later covered by Elvis) in 1953: "Hound Dog." At the time of this photo, she was probably on tour with Johnny Ace. She died in 1984.

p 61, bottom

Ace shot himself while playing Russian roulette backstage at a 1954 Christmas Eve show in Houston, Texas. He was on tour with Big Mama Thornton at the time.

"That's Johnny Ace waving. That was at Hernando and Calhoun….I arranged Johnny Ace's funeral for Don Robey, secured Clayborne Temple, and got Gatemouth Moore to preach."

p 62

Fulson's 1950 hit, "Every Day I Have the Blues," was written by Memphis Slim and later became associated with B. B. King. King's first hit record was a cover of Fulson's "Three O'Clock Blues" from 1951. Born in 1921, Fulson died in 1999.

"No, he [re: the audience member in suspenders on far right] don't come off the fields. Not straight to a nightclub on Beale Street. Men got dressed up!"

p 63

Ray Charles was born in Albany, Georgia, in 1930. He toured as a singer with the Lowell Fulson Band in the early 1950s and was the arranger on Guitar Slim's 1953 hit, "The Things That I Used to Do." This is around the time of his own first R & B hit—1955's "I've Got a Woman"—which marked the emergence of his distinctive, gospel-influenced vocals.

pp 64-65: (Left to right): King, James Walker, Benita Coles, Earl Forrest, Evelyn Young, Cato Walker, unidentified, "Sleepy" Jerry Smith, Ted Curry, Millar "Mother" Lee, Floyd Newman, Kenny Sands, Calvin Owens, Richard Lillie, Laurence Birdine, Paul Pinkman, Frank Brown.

"The horns give me the harmonies I first heard in church, and the rhythm section locks me into grooves that satisfy my soul." —B. B. King on his band

p 66

(Left to right): Unidentified, King, John, Pigmeat Markham (comedian), two unidentifieds. Little Willie John, born in Arkansas in 1937, was discovered by Johnny Otis. His 1956 hit, "Fever," was later covered by Peggy Lee. He followed it with, among others, "Talk to Me, Talk to Me" (1958). John went to prison for knifing a man in 1966 and died there in 1968.

"You know, it's sad when you

look—how a guy lives and dies. He was quite a little fellow."

p 67, top

(Left to right): Brown Berry (electric bass), Robert Reed, unidentified, Earl Malone, unidentified, Jett Bledsoe (at the mike).

"The Spirit of Memphis, the Soul Stirrers, the Five Blind Boys, all of them were a collection of great, cross-country quartets….Used to have great musical settings in the Mason temple."

p 67, bottom

(Far left, with trophy): Willie Gordon, director and singer with the Pattersonaires, a Memphis gospel group.

"This is the same church where Aretha's father, C. L. Franklin, got his start preaching. Aretha and Sam Cooke regarded this church choir as one of their early influences."

p 68

Roebuck "Pop" Staples, Mavis, Purvis, and Cleotha. Pop, born in Winona, Mississippi, in 1915, learned his guitar style from the most famous Delta bluesmen. He formed his family singing group in 1953 in Chicago. They cut only gospel music in the 1950s (when this picture was made), later moving to socially conscious, gospel-influenced soul, such as "Respect Yourself" (1971). Pop died in 2000.

"They were highly honored, Pop Staples and them, every time they came."

p 69

Ernestine Hooks, wife of Robert Hooks, handing a record to Martelle LaGroan, and an unidentified.

"One thing about African American families: there always was pride."

p 70

"[Laura Dukes] was even a greater singer than Lillie Mae Glover, but she just wasn't as photogenic."

p 71

"Distributors, jukebox operators, and retailers knew that white teenagers were picking up on the feel of the black music. These people liked the plays and the sales they were getting, but they were concerned: 'We're afraid our children might fall in love with black people.'"
—Sam Phillips of Sun Records

p 72

Born Herman Parker in West Memphis in 1927, Junior Parker played harmonica with Sonny Boy Williamson on KWEM in 1948 and the next year with Howlin' Wolf and Ike Turner. His first hit was 1953's "Feelin' Good" on Sun Records, which he followed with "Mystery Train" (later covered by Elvis Presley). Parker died in 1971.

"That's Junior Parker when he first popped. That's my coat he had on, my tie, and my watch. He wanted a dressed-up picture. He was Al Green's cousin."

p 73

"Nobody but the people of Beale Street knew Fred. He hung out at Red Johnny's and on Beale Street between the Hotel Men's Improvement Club and the Elks Club. He never had any strong, controlled audience, but if he ever had a chance to get up and play his harp, he'd pull it out, and he played it."

p 75

The Sparrow was a WDIA on-air personality whose real name was Solomon Hardy. WDIA increased its power from 250 watts to 50,000 watts in June 1954, reaching a million and a half black listeners in Arkansas, Mississippi, Missouri, and Tennessee.

"When WDIA went 50,000 watts, that's what blew the top! We were getting letters from all over, far as the station would reach."
—Jett Bledsoe of the Spirit of Memphis

p 76

(Left to right): Prentis Barnes, Peter Graves, Bobby Lest, Harvey Fuqua (lead). The Moonglows' big hit was "Sincerely" in 1955. Fuqua later became director of Motown's artist development department and was instrumental in signing one of the later Moonglows, Marvin Gaye. (In back-

ground: WDIA's Martha Jean the Queen dressed as "Princess Premium Stuff" and WDIA's Robert "Honeymoon" Garner as "Moon Honey.")

p 77

Carla Thomas (in headband, facing camera). The story line for the 1956 Goodwill Revue was that "Indians" were taking over the auditorium. WDIA's A. C. "Moohah" Williams played "Big Chief," upset that his tribe was attracted to this "new" music, rock and roll.

"[Elvis] was young and he was not chaperoned by Colonel Parker and them around black people. That was his own hobbyistic style—of coming around African-American people."

p 78

Presley's first movie, *Love Me Tender*, was just out. His 1956 hits on RCA included "Heartbreak Hotel" and his cover of Big Mama Thornton's "Hound Dog." Three nights earlier, Elvis had stopped by Sun Records for an impromptu sing-along with Johnny Cash, Jerry Lee Lewis, and Carl Perkins that came to be known as the Million Dollar Quartet. In explaining Presley's success, Withers notes the growing importance of television and comments, "You had hearing—plus hearing and seeing." At the time, King was earning from $500 to $700 a day touring.

p 79, top left

Benton, born Benjamin Franklin Peay in 1931, was a respected R & B singer with "A Million Miles from Nowhere" out in 1956. This was Presley's second and last appearance at a Goodwill Revue. His 1957 hits included "Jailhouse Rock" and "All Shook Up." He was about ten days away from receiving his draft notice from the army.

p 79, top right

Parker had taken over Johnny Ace's band after Ace's death and was touring with Bland. Bland, born in 1930 in Rosemark, Tennessee, had the first of many national bestsellers, "Farther On up the Road," in 1957. About the music he listened to this night from the wings, Presley commented, "It was the real thing—basic. Right from the heart."

p 79, bottom left

Monroe, WDIA's first black woman DJ, hosted the very successful "Tan Town Homemaker's Show." She was a Beale Street legend.

> "There weren't any divas in 1950—especially black ones—but Willa Monroe, honey, was a diva....She would be laid out on a chaise lounge, like Marilyn Monroe or Mae West or something."
> —Natolyn Williams, Nat Dee's daughter

p 80

With WDIA's Martha Jean Steinberg and Robert Thomas as "Crazy Man Crazy."Charles's 1956 hits included "Drown in My Own Tears," "Hallelujah, I Love Her So," and "Lonely Avenue." By this time, he was a major star, and his

seven-piece band was already a model for R & B ensembles.

p 81

After Phillips hit with Presley, Gordon was the last black artist on Sun. The 1956 single he's promoting here, "The Chicken (Dance with You)," was the prototype for Rufus Thomas's 1970 Stax hit, "Do the Funky Chicken."

p 82, top

Hudson hosted "A Date with Ruby" on WHHM. Phillips, born Esther Mae Jones in 1935, was another artist discovered by Johnny Otis. Her first hit, "Double Crossing Blues," came in 1950 while she was still a teenager. Later in her career, she scored with her version of "What a Difference a Day Makes." She died in 1984.

> "You had in Memphis WDIA, WCBR, WHBQ, WHHM, WMC, and WREC."

p 82, bottom

(Left to right): Erskine Hawkins, Hamilton, Clifford Miller and wife. Hawkin's was a trumpet player and big band leader. Roy Hamilton died in 1969, at age forty. His most notable hits include "You'll Never Walk Alone" in 1954, "Unchained Melody" in 1955, and "Don't Let Go" in 1958.

> "Clifford Miller was the owner of the Flamingo Club in downtown Memphis. Miller was undergirded by Bob Berrelman, who was a white club owner south of Memphis in Mississippi."

p 83

Led by Clyde Leopard (drums), the Snearly Ranch Boys were the house band at the Cotton Club. They recorded briefly at Sun Records. Members would include Jim Stewart, founder of Stax, and steel guitarist Stan Kessler, author of hits such as "I Forgot to Remember to Forget" and "I'm Left You're Right She's Gone."

p 84, top

> "Evelyn Young was a lady who blew alto. Evelyn was fierce. We called her Mama Nuts and she could flat-out play anything. A lot of the younger saxists in Memphis who went on to stardom, musicians like Hank Crawford, will tell you Evelyn shaped their style."
> —B. B. King

p 84, bottom

Reverend Bell (center), Clara Ward (to his right), Gertrude Ward, with glasses (to his left), lead singer Marion Williams (far right). The Ward Singers became gospel headliners in 1943. Clara Ward heavily influenced Aretha Franklin. Williams, one of gospel's greatest singers, led on Brewster's "Surely God Is Able" in 1950.

p 85

(Left to right): M. M. Watson, a Memphis socialite; classical voice teacher Madame MacLieve; Anderson; WDIA's Willa Monroe (conducting the interview).

Anderson was born in Philadelphia in 1897. A legendary opera singer and major box-office draw, she was denied permission to sing at Washington, D.C.'s Constitution Hall in 1939, eliciting a wave of nationwide protests. She received the Presidential Medal of Freedom in 1963 and died in 1993.

> "This was at Union Station as they came out of the segregated side and had the press conference in the parking lot. But still freedom!"

p 86

(Left to right): Nick Adams, actor, friend of Presley's (and James Dean's), and star of TV's The Rebel; Guy Lansky; Presley; Bernard Lansky. The Lanskys opened their clothing store on Beale Street in 1946 and became one of the main sources of black fashion styles in Memphis.

> "If I had gone the dozens of times that the Lansky Brothers called me to come up to Beale Street and Second because Elvis was coming down, I would have a high reservoir of Elvis's early life pictures. But they were not given to paying."

p 87

Born in 1942, Lymon was twelve when he recorded "Why Do Fools Fall in Love?" with the Teenagers. He went solo in 1957 and died of a drug overdose in 1968. (Note that the girl on the right is wearing a Frankie Lymon necklace and skirt.)

> "What did I want? What would any kid of thirteen want?"
> —Frankie Lymon

p 88

Bland had thirty-six R & B bestsellers between 1957 and 1970.

"It was 1957 before I got a style of my own….I was listening to Reverend C. L. Franklin a lot at the time, [his sermon] 'The Eagle Stirreth Her Nest,' and that's where I got my squall from."
—Bobby Blue Bland

p 89

"No special lighting. I just got a hard shadow."

p 90

Benton's first major hit, "It's Just a Matter of Time," came in 1958, the same year he wrote "A Lover's Question" for Clyde McPhatter. He would go on to record top singles, including "The Boll Weevil Song" (1961) and "A Rainy Night in Georgia" (1970).

p 91

Banks was born in 1941 in Memphis and started as a gospel singer. He became a writer for Stax, including Johnnie Taylor's "Who's Making Love," the Staple Singers' "Be What You Are," and Isaac Hayes's "If Loving You Is Wrong (I Don't Want to Be Right)." Garner graduated from Manassas High School, was one of the original Teen Tone Singers at WDIA, and became one of the station's on-air personalities in 1954.

pp 92–93

"That Club Ebony was the same as The Hippodrome. The Hippodrome first, and then it became the Club Ebony. These people are waiting for a *Tri-State Defender* Home Show. This is *not* a club audience."

p 94

Behind Charles is Hank Crawford, Charles's bandleader. Crawford was born in Memphis in 1934 and was a schoolhood friend of Phineas Newborn, Jr., and Frank Strozier. His nickname, "Hank," was in honor of Memphis sax legend Hank O'Day. Crawford played with the Ben Branch and Tuff Green bands before he joined Charles in 1958. He went on to become a jazz star in his own right, cutting twelve albums with his own group between 1960 and 1970.

"He's [Hank Crawford] a Memphis boy."

p 95

(Left to right): Boots Coke, the original bass player for the Gentrys, who scored with "Keep On Dancing," J. B. Smith, unidentified, Merlin Smith, Wayne Crook.

p 96

Reed's highly influential urban blues included "You Don't Have to Go" (1955), "Ain't That Loving You Baby" (1956), "Baby, What You Want Me to Do?" and

"Bright Lights, Big City" (both 1960). He was born in Mississippi in 1925 and died in 1976.

p 97

Wolf was born Chester Arthur Burnett in West Point, Mississippi, in 1910. A blues singer with an enormous, rough voice, he performed on street corners through the 1930s, had his first band in Memphis in the 1940s, and appeared on the West Memphis station KWEM in 1950. Wolf recorded at Sun Records in 1951 before moving to Chicago in 1952, where he hooked up with the Chess label. He died in 1976.

p 98

Wolf is singing "Spoonful," his 1960 hit. That same year, he had "Back Door Man" and "Wang Dang Doodle," all sexually charged "deep" blues.

p 99

(Left to right): Unidentified, B. B. King, Howlin' Wolf, Muddy Waters, Ivory Joe Hunter. Blues legend Muddy Waters was born McKinley Morganfield in Rolling Fork, Mississippi, in 1915. His career started with the Silas Green Tent Show ca. 1940. He moved to Chicago in 1943, where his numerous Chess hits included "Honey Bee" in 1951 and "Got My Mojo Workin'" in 1954. Waters crossed over to a white audience, playing the Newport Folk Festival in 1960. He died in 1983. Hunter, born in 1914, died in Memphis in 1974. His hits included "I Almost Lost My Mind" (1950) and "Since I Met You Baby" (1956). WDIA sponsored the city's first black little league teams in 1955 with funds from the Goodwill Revues.

p 100

Little Walter was widely acclaimed as the blues' greatest harmonica player. Born Marion Walter Jacobs in 1930, he moved to Chicago in 1947, where he joined the Muddy Waters band. The year after going solo in 1952, he hit with "Sad Hours," "Mean Old World," and "Blues with a Feeling." He died in 1968. Cotton, also a harmonica player, was born in Tunica, Mississippi, in 1935. He began performing with Sonny Boy Williamson in 1945, cut "Cotton Crop Blues" at Sun Records in 1950, and was playing with Howlin' Wolf in and around Memphis in the early part of that decade. He moved to Chicago to play in the Muddy Waters band in the mid-1950s and became a solo act at the beginning of the 1960s.

"So Muddy Waters walked up to me and said, 'Is you James Cotton?' and I said, 'Yeah' and he said, 'I'm Muddy Waters,' and I said, 'Yeah, and I'm Jesus Christ.'"
—James Cotton

p 101

(Left to right): Unidentified, Chico Chism, James Cotton, Little Walter, Howlin' Wolf, Big Bill Hill.

"They hired me. They were trying to get a picture of [Wolf] in *Jet*. They hired me to go all the way to Little Rock with him to take some pictures in a cotton field. They paid me nice little money: fifty, sixty, a hundred dollars. And it never appeared in *Jet*."

p 102

King became famous as a stinging, left-handed blues guitarist, but he started out playing drums for Jimmy Reed. Born in Indianola, Mississippi, in 1923, it wasn't until 1961 that he hit with "Don't Throw Your Love on Me Too Strong."

"Club Paradise, of course, was a defunct bowling alley that was over on Orleans. You could give a big show at Club Paradise that you couldn't give at Club Handy. Had 250 tables. Headed by Sunbeam Mitchell and financed by Abe Plough."

p 103

Parker toured with Bland throughout the early 1960s, when his hits included "Driving Wheel" and "In the Dark."

p 104

Bates published the *Arkansas State Gazette*. His wife, Daisy, organized the school integration drive in Little Rock in 1957. Franklin was born in Memphis in 1942 and grew up singing gospel music in Detroit. She crossed over to secular music and first played New York's Apollo Theater just before this picture was made. Cooke, born in Clarksdale, Mississippi, in 1931, was raised in Chicago. As a gospel star, he often stayed with the Franklins in Detroit. After "You Send Me" in 1957, he had a string of hits including (in 1960) "Only Sixteen," "Wonderful World," and "Chain Gang."

p 105

Ike Turner was born in Clarksdale, Mississippi, in 1931. He produced for Sam Phillips at Sun Records at the start of the 1950s and played with Howlin' Wolf in the mid-1950s. The first Ike and Tina record, "A Fool in Love," was released in 1960, followed by "It's Gonna Work Out Fine." Tina Turner, born Annie Mae Bullock in

Brownsville, Tennessee, in 1938 married Turner in 1958. The pair's hits included "Proud Mary" (1971).

pp 106–107

The Ike and Tina Turner Revue, a major R & B act, consisted of nine musicians and three background singers: the Ikettes.

p 108

Thomas, born in Memphis in 1942, is the daughter of Rufus Thomas. She cut her first hit, "Gee Whiz," while on vacation from college in 1961. She continued to record with Stax, including "Tramp," a bestselling duet with Otis Redding from 1967.

"Oh, Carla Thomas is a great image. She was as beautiful as she could be."

p 109

Burke was a boy preacher and gospel singer born in Philadelphia in 1936. His first pop hit was "Just Out of Reach" in 1961, followed by "Got to Get You Off of My Mind" (1965). Burke, still touring, often performed in a gold tuxedo.

pp 110-111

Brown was born in Barnwell, Tennessee, in 1933. His first national R & B hit was "Try Me" in 1958. His LP *Live at the Apollo*, vol. 2, sold a million copies in 1960. Among the Godfather of Soul's many hits was

1965's "Papa's Got a Brand New Bag."

"I developed my cape routine after watching the wrestler Gorgeous George on television….I usually lost eight or nine pounds a show."
—James Brown

p 112

Overton Vertis Wright was born in Leno, Tennessee, in 1939. He died in 1980. Wright sang gospel with the Spirit of Memphis and the Sunset Travelers. His plaintive, soul-wrenching vocals helped make hits out of "That's How Strong My Love Is" in 1964 and "Eight Men, Four Women" in 1965, but he remained something of a Memphis cult figure.

"He lived and died early in life. Came out of the gospel music into pop and parlayed big."

p 113

Carr was an eccentric, deeply talented singer, born in Memphis in 1942. He would often appear in the recording studio and then refuse to sing. His signature numbers included "You've Got My Mind Messed Up" and "Dark End of the Street" from 1966. He died in 2001.

p 114

Jackson was the most familiar representative of gospel music to many Americans. Born in 1911 in New Orleans, she moved to Chicago in 1927, and among her biggest hits was Reverend Brewster's "Move On Up a Little Higher" in 1947. Mahalia, as she was known to millions, died in 1972.

p 115

Franklin, twenty-six, had just cut her groundbreaking *Respect* album in Muscle Shoals, Alabama.

p 116

Cooke was shot in a motel in Los Angeles; his wake at A. R. Leek's funeral home in Chicago drew more than six thousand mourners.

"Sam Cooke was a very personal friend of mine."

p 117

"That was just a little comin'-up group that had a studio sitting."

p 118, top

Domingo Samudio was born in Dallas, Texas, in 1937. As Sam the Sham, he and his band, the Pharaohs, recorded "Wooly Bully" in Sam Phillips's studio in Memphis in 1965. Produced by Stan Kessler (of the Snearly Ranch Boys), it eventually went to #2 on the charts and was followed by "Lil' Red Riding Hood" (1966), among others.

"This is all the way from yesterday and into tomorrow, to the rock and soul of today."

p 118, bottom

(Left to right): Carla Thomas, Dee Clark,

Price, Martha Jean Steinberg, unidentified, Howlin' Wolf. Clark, born in 1938, is best known for the 1961 hit "Raindrops." Price's hits include "Lawdy Miss Clawdy" (1952) and, in 1959, "Stagger Lee" and "Personality."

p 119

Jones was born in Memphis in 1944 and was recognized as a talented musician before he graduated from high school. He played sax and bass with Willie Mitchell's band at the Flamingo Room and became the organ player and leader of Booker T. and the MG's in 1962 at age eighteen. Jones stayed with Stax until 1969 and still tours with the MG's.

"Booker T. was a younger boy, younger than the peer group he was with. A young, ingenious musician."

p 120

(Standing rear, left to right): Ben Cauley, Carl Cunningham, Ronnie Caldwell, Jimmie King, James Alexander; (front) Phalon Jones, Redding. Redding, one of the key figures in modern soul music, was born in Georgia in 1941 and died in 1967. His first hit with Stax's Volt label, "These Arms of Mine," came in 1962. In 1967, as he scored with the Carla Thomas duet "Tramp," he also played the Monterey Pop Festival and began to cross over to a wider audience. The Bar-Kays began as a local Memphis band called the Imperials and cut their hit "Soul Finger" in 1967. All but Alexander and Cauley were killed in a plane crash on December 10, 1967.

"Ben Cauley, he fell clear. Alexander was on another plane with Otis's wife; he lived. The five in the center were killed. That's my cousin's son, Phalon Jones."

p 122

(Left to right): Pervis, Mavis, Pop, Cleo. The Staple Singers signed with Stax in July 1968, four months after Dr. King's death. "Respect Yourself" was a hit in 1971; "I'll Take You There" in 1972.

"We visited Dr. King's church in Montgomery before the movement actually got started. When we heard Dr. King preach, we went back to the motel and had a meeting. Pops said, 'Now, if he can preach this, we can sing it.'"
—Mavis Staples

p 123

(Rear, standing): "Big" Perkins (Boss Crump's family chauffeur), Ben Branch; (seated) Coretta Scott King, Aretha Franklin.

"Aretha came here in support of the SCLC convention after the assassination of Martin King. Her daddy, the Reverend Franklin, came here, and she came with him."

p 124

Including James Alexander and Harry Henderson (far left), singer Larry Dotson (front with cigarette), WLOK DJ Melvin "A-Cookin'" Jones (far right). The Bar-Kays re-formed in 1968 and backed Isaac Hayes on "Hot Buttered Soul" (1969) and "Theme from *Shaft*" (1971).

p 125

With Josephine Bridges, producer of the

Temprees on Stax's We Produce label. Taylor, born in Arkansas in 1938, replaced Sam Cooke as lead singer in the gospel Soul Stirrers in 1957. He recorded on Cooke's SAR label in 1963 and signed with Stax in 1965 after Cooke's death. "Who's Making Love" in 1968 sold two million copies (written by the We Three songwriting team including Homer Banks). Taylor died in 2000.

"Jo Bridges was the first image I used to advertise my business. She was a little girl in my neighborhood. Her grandfather, I was his paper boy."

p 126

(Left to right): Unidentified, Roosevelt Jamison (James Carr's manager), unidentified, Butler, local physician Dr. Horn, unidentified, Memphis attorney Seymour Rosenberg. Butler's first hit was "For Your Precious Love" (1957) with Curtis Mayfield and the Impressions. Born in Sunflower, Mississippi, in 1939, he moved to Chicago in 1942. His string of soul hits include "He Will Break Your Heart" (1960). Butler cowrote "I've Been Lovin' You Too Long (to Stop Now)" with Otis Redding in 1965 and signed a distribution deal with Stax in 1969.

p 127

Little Milton Campbell was born in Mississippi in 1934. He recorded with Ike Turner at Sun Records in 1953, and his 1965 hits were "We're Gonna Make It" and "Who's Cheatin' Who." Little Milton signed with Stax in 1971, where "That's What Love Will Make You Do" scored the next year. B.B.'s single "The Thrill Is Gone" reignited his career in 1970. Albert King signed with Stax in 1966, where he cut the classic *Born Under a Bad Sign* LP with Booker T. and the MG's.

p 128

After Ross's many hits with the Supremes—from "Where Did Our Love Go" (1964) to "Someday We'll Be Together" (1969)—she broke with the group about when this picture was made. Her first solo hit was "Reach Out and Touch Somebody's Hand" in 1970.

"This was a big day in Mississippi honoring Charles Evers [mayor of Fayette, brother of Medgar Evers]."

p 129

Robinson sang gospel with the Roberta Martin Singers, was in Memphis in 1950, and signed with Peacock Records in 1953, but was perhaps best known as the host of his nationally seen TV gospel show. Born in Canton, Mississippi, in 1932, he died in 1998.

"[Record companies and promoters exploited] the art and its artists for the money, then put very little money back into the art to strengthen and make it more popular."
—Rev. Cleophus Robinson explaining the weakening of gospel music in the late 1960s

p 130

Hayes, born in Covington, Tennessee, in 1942, went to Manassas High School, sang with gospel and doo-wop groups, and in 1961 with the Ben Branch Band at Club Tropicana. He made his first recording in 1962 and went to Stax in 1964. Sidney Kirk (second from left) went on to play keyboards with Hayes. He was the son of "Spoon" Kirk, a Beale Street barrel-house piano player.

"They were coming to be, coming to be."

p 131

Porter, born in Memphis in 1941, went to Booker T. Washington High School and played at the Elks Club with Booker T. Jones (of MG's fame). Porter became a songwriter, working with Isaac Hayes at Stax in 1964. The team wrote "Hold On! I'm Comin'" (1966), "Soul Man," and "When Something Is Wrong with My Baby" (1967), among many others.

"David Porter and Isaac Hayes were the launchers of Sam and Dave. David Porter was one of the icons of Stax."

p 132

Helen Washington in rear. Hayes's *Hot Buttered Soul* LP sold a million copies in 1969, followed by *The Isaac Hayes Movement* in 1970. His touring band, the Isaac Hayes Movement, included an eight-piece rhythm section, an eight-piece horn section, four female background vocalists, and seven "interpretive dancers" headed by Washington.

p 133

Washington, David Porter's niece, was released from Tennessee State Prison on the basis of a letter from Isaac Hayes and became his lead dancer.

p 134

(Left to right): Smith, Al Bell's cousin and Stax executive; Thomas, whose Stax hits include "Walking the Dog" (1963) and "Do

the Funky Chicken" (1970); Bill Russell, Boston Celtics basketball great.

p 135

Ingram, born in Jackson, Tennessee, in 1944, went to Stax in 1968. He often opened for Isaac Hayes, cowrote "Respect Yourself" for the Staple Singers, and hit with "[If Loving You Is Wrong] I Don't Want to Be Right" in 1972.

"Be good to me, baby."

p 136

Green, born in Forrest City, Arkansas, in 1946, moved to Grand Rapids, Michigan, in 1959 and had a small hit with "Back Up Train" in 1966. Green met Willie Mitchell in Midland, Texas, in 1968, signed with Hi Records in 1969, and a year and a half later struck gold with "Tired of Being Alone" and "Let's Stay Together." These were followed by many other hits, including 1972's "I'm Still in Love with You."

p 137

Mitchell, born in Ashland, Mississippi, in 1928, played with the Tuff Green and Al Jackson, Sr., bands in high school. A mainstay of Memphis music, he was on B. B. King's first recordings, and his own band in the mid-1950s would include Phineas Newborn, Jr., Frank Strozier, Al Jackson, Jr., and many others. He signed with Hi Records in 1961 and hit with the instrumentals "20-75" (1964) and "Soul Serenade" (1968). As a producer, Mitchell worked with Roy Brown, O. V. Wright, Bobby Blue Bland, and, most famously, Al Green.

"Willie Mitchell came up, and he picked some of these fruits of [Memphis] music."

p 138

"Al Green was commemorated by the city. They did a commemorative to him and his mother. Had an Al Green Day at the Coliseum. Al Green's church is off Elvis Presley [Boulevard]. I go there on Sundays to worship."

p 139

Mitchell on horn; his brother James on sax.

"It's the laziness of the rhythm. You hear those old lazy horns half a beat behind the music, and you think they're gonna miss it, and all of a sudden, just so lazy, they come in and start to sway with it."
—Willie Mitchell, explaining the Memphis beat

p 140, right

"Jimmy Stewart was a banker; he was a real organizer. Of course what happened was after he organized, then some of the wise California art thieves came in here and began to show people like Al Bell and some of the other noted artists that they didn't need Jimmy Stewart."

p 142

William Bell hit with "You Don't Miss Your Water [Till Your Well Runs Dry]" in 1962,

the year he came to Stax. He was born William Yarborough in Memphis in 1939, worked as lead singer with the Del Rios at the Plantation Inn, and sang with Phineas Newborn, Sr., at the Flamingo Room. Al Bell was born Alvertis Isbell in Brinkley, Arkansas, in 1940. He started out as a DJ, worked on WLOK in 1961, and then was hired as promotion man at Stax in 1965. By 1970, he'd emerged as co-owner of the label and was sole owner by 1972. Three years later, he was indicted for fraudulent bank loans. He was acquitted in 1976. Ekstine signed with Stax in 1969 and recorded four albums there.

"They brought charges against Bell—conspiracy and all that bullshit—and it destroyed the man. And it helped destroy the company in the process."
—Jim Stewart

p 143

Stax closed its doors January 12, 1976 by order of a federal bankruptcy court judge.

p 144

With A. C. "Moohaw" Williams (on right), leading WDIA personality and organizer of the Teen Tone Singers. Jackie "Moms" Mabley was born in 1897. A well-known and beloved comedian, she began her career playing the Harlem Cotton Club in the 1920s and cowrote the Broadway hit "Fast and Furious" with Zora Neale Hurston in 1931. She died in 1975.

p146

Ray Charles's backup singers.

p 147

As well as being the great writer and performer of jazz classics such as "Mood Indigo" and "Sophisticated Lady," Ellington, born in 1899, wrote many symphonic works and, late in his astonishing career, often played with symphonies. He died in 1974. The cellist is Vincent DeFrank, director of the Memphis Symphony.

p 148

The big band leader and jazz legend was born William Basie in 1904, played in Kansas City in the thirties, and started his own band in 1935. His "Every Day I Have the Blues," sung by Joe Williams, was a number-two R & B hit in 1955. Basie died in 1984.

p 149

(Left to right): Cato Walker, B. B. King's bus driver. Dizzy Gillespie, the be-bop jazz legend, born John Birks Gillespie in 1917, died in 1983. Gene "Bowlegs" Miller, trumpet player and leader of a Memphis band that included the young Isaac Hayes and Andrew Love, later of the Memphis Horns. Bowlegs played behind James Carr and Otis Redding, among many others.

p 150

Simon's mix of soul and country-western sounds hit with "Drowning in the Sea of Love" in 1971 and "Power of Love" the next year. Simon sang at his friend's, Otis Redding's, funeral.

p 151

Pride is one of few successful black country singers in the modern era. He was born in Sledge, Mississippi, in 1938 and played baseball with the Memphis Red Sox in the Negro Leagues in the early 1950s. By 1967, he was appearing at the Grand Ol' Opry. His many hits include "Kiss an Angel Good Mornin'" (1971).

"This was at a little restaurant. This guy was a doctor—who was enthused."

p 152

Dionne Warwick's soulful pop hits include "Don't Make Me Over" in 1963 and "Walk On By" from the next year. Born in 1941, she tried recording at Chip Moman's American Studio in Memphis in 1969 without much success. But more hits followed, including 1970's "I'll Never Fall in Love Again."

"That's Whitney Houston's aunt."

p 154

"Lillie Mae Glover, her greatest days was her last days, in that she took on the Ma Rainey title. Her strongest image of performance was in Blues Alley [off Monroe Street] in the last round of her life."

p 155

"Big Ella was a big personality on Beale Street. She was converted into religion in her last years. She got away from blues singing."

pp 156–157: Lewis, born in 1935, and Rich, born in 1932, both began as rock-a-billy stars on Sun Records. Lewis's first hit was "Whole Lotta Shakin' Goin' On" from 1957, and Rich's was in 1960: "Lonely Week-ends." Both went on to major country-western careers. Rich, perhaps best known for 1973's "Behind Closed Doors," died in 1984.

p 158

Flack is best known for "The First Time Ever I Saw Your Face" from 1972 and "Killing Me Softly with His Song" (1973).

p 159

Thomas was born Muzyad Yakhoob in 1914. A comedian and television personality, he was the major fund-raiser for St. Jude's Hospital for Children in Memphis, which opened in 1962. (To his left, with cane) Matthew Thornton, Sr.

"Matthew Thornton was a very personal friend of Mr. Handy. He was a special delivery mailman in his career....He was just a part of the popular vernacular: the mayor of Beale Street before I was coming to Beale Street. Old Man Thornton was a man of stature, an image of prominence and decency....That's one of his grandchildren."

p 160

With his stepmother, Lilly Chatman. Memphis Slim was born Peter Chatman in Memphis in 1915. A world-renowned blues piano player, his career began at the Midway Cafe at Fourth and Beale in 1931. He moved to Chicago in 1939, where he appeared with Big Bill Broonzy. In 1948, he wrote "Every Day I Have the Blues," which became a hit for Lowell Fulson and one of B. B. King's signature songs. He emigrated to Europe in the early 1960s and didn't return to Memphis until 1978, ten years before his death.

**"[I am] bitter—no, scornful—about the place accorded me and black bluesmen in America."
—Memphis Slim**

p 161

"B.B. is a man who feeds off the audience, plus feeds in the audience. And he has the strongest sense of humbleness of anyone that you'll ever meet."

Dancing in the aisles, City Auditorium, mid-1960s.